The Dictionary of Event Management

Joe Jeff Goldblatt, CSEP, MTA
Carol F. McKibben, CSEP
Editors
in conjunction with
The International Special Events Society (ISES)

Foreword by James E. Jones, V.P. and G.M.,
Marquis Events International by Marriott

VAN NOSTRAND REINHOLD
I(T)P® A Division of International Thomson Publishing Inc.

New York • Albany • Bonn • Boston • Detroit • London • Madrid • Melbourne
Mexico City • Paris • San Francisco • Singapore • Tokyo • Toronto

Copyright © 1996 by Van Nostrand Reinhold

ITP A division of International Thomson Publishing, Inc.
The ITP Logo is a registered trademark under license

Printed in the United States of America

For more information, contact:

Van Nostrand Reinhold
115 Fifth Avenue
New York, NY 10003

Chapman & Hall GmbH
Pappelallee 3
69469 Weinheim
Germany

Chapman & Hall
2-6 Boundary Row
London
SE1 8HN
United Kingdom

International Thomson Publishing Asia
221 Henderson Road #05–10
Henderson Building
Singapore 0315

Thomas Nelson Australia
102 Dodds Street
South Melbourne 3205
Victoria, Australia

International Thomson Publishing Japan
Hirakawacho Kyowa Building, 3F
2–2–1 Hirakawacho
Chiyada-ku, 102 Tokyo
Japan

Nelson Canada
1120 Birchmount Road
Scarborough, Ontario
Canada, M1K 5G4

International Thomson Editores
Seneca 53
Col. Polanco
11560 Mexico D.F. Mexico

All rights reserved. No part of this work covered by the copyright hereon may be reproduced or used in any form or by any means—graphic, electronic, or mechanical, including photocopying, recording, taping, or information storage and retrieval systems—without the written permission of the publisher.

ISBN 0-442-02349-9

Dedication

There's a *soul* to the events industry that isn't about making money. It's about creating memories and happiness. It's about helping other people and organizations achieve their goals, and it's about the celebration of life. This work is dedicated to event professionals around the world who do this work because it is in their souls to do it and to those who have stopped along the way to teach and train others. And this work is for the students, both now and to come, who will find the *soul* of this industry and make it their own.

Foreword

The editors of the first dictionary of event management deserve hearty congratulations from the entire special events industry, its members and those students and individuals who will enter the special events industry in the future. The outstanding team that produced this important new book has accomplished something that for years has been a much needed tool in the development of the industry: a common language.

This industry, as you know, has taken a life and career path of it's own. Combined with the editors' previous books and journals serving the industry, Joe Goldblatt and Carol McKibben have now provided a much needed missing link.

The Dictionary of Event Management should be at the desk of every student, special events beginner, marketing and operations specialist, and special events industry professional as the one source of information and meaning. The entire special events industry owes the editors a debt of gratitude for this important undertaking. They have secured information that was henceforth unavailable in any one place. This unique reference tool introduces both classic terminology with the latest Internet vocabulary to cover the breadth and depth of this fast growing profession. Whether you are in search of the translation of one of the industry acronyms or wish to clarify the usage for a technical term when ordering lighting, sound, or special effects, you will now be able to turn to one comprehensive source.

This book unifies the special events industry through a common language and therefore improves our practice and in doing so, our service to our customers. You can be assured that it will be in the top left corner of my book shelf and I will show it to all of my clients. I am certain you will as well.

James E. Jones
Vice President & General Manager
Marquis Events International by Marriott

Preface

The Dictionary of Event Management attempts to fill a gap in the events industry. When we entered the profession well over a decade ago, it lacked cohesion, and resources were scattered and difficult to locate. We have made it our goal to provide those missing resources. When the Certified Special Events Professional (CSEP) designation was created by the International Special Events Society (ISES), we involved ourselves in its development and earned the designation. In that process we found that students and event professionals need a reference for terminology. To meet that need we have created the book you hold today.

The Dictionary of Event Management is the first of its kind, and it encompasses more than 1,800 entries from the field of event management and draws on terminology from audiovisual technology, catering, communications, computer networking, decorating, entertainment, environmental and floral design, food and beverage service, laser effects, lighting, meeting planning, pyrotechnics, rental, risk management, special effects, tenting, and travel.

It is meant to be used as a dictionary and has been validated by International Special Events Society (ISES) members in the United States, Canada, and Australia. Canada and Australia were chosen to represent international validation because of their large numbers of ISES members.

The characteristics of this resource may be briefly summarized:

1. The dictionary format is followed throughout with all entries listed in alphabetical order.

2. Terms that have synonymous meanings are referenced to each other. Synonyms immediately follow the meaning. The expression *also known as* provides optional terminology and reference, and *See* refers the reader to another term for reference.

3. A pronunciation guide follows the term for those words that are difficult to pronounce.

Preface

4. Every acronym appears in parenthesis immediately after the associated term and is also included in alphabetical order throughout the dictionary; each is cross-referenced to its complete term.

5. **Boldface** directs the reader to terms to be found in the dictionary.

6. *Italics* indicates variations on terms found in the dictionary.

Because the event management field is comprised of so much diversified technology, this resource can provide you with:

1. a quick and easy reference to terminology that spans the operations and marketing segments you need to utilize;

2. immediate and practical assistance when you are planning events or writing proposals;

3. a handy resource for training new employees and a quick-reference guide to use as a refresher;

4. a guide for students and candidates seeking the Certified Special Events Professional (CSEP) designation; and

5. a comprehensive listing of **Internet** terms ... The Internet is the hottest new venue for special events.

This is only the beginning. Technology is changing so rapidly that it is impossible to keep up with its evolution. Even though we've had the terminology validated by top professionals, we still invite your comments and written suggestions and regret if we have missed important terms that should be included.

As the top professionals in our field know, learning is an ongoing process. We hope that this book will add to your learning and that you will find it useful every day, at work or study.

Acknowledgments

Many hands have joined together to produce this comprehensive dictionary of event management. The many resources of The George Washington University School of Business and Public Management International Institute for Tourism Studies, Educational Services Institute, and The George Washington University Event Management Certificate Program in Washington, D.C., enabled the researchers to research, test, and validate these terms. Our colleagues of the International Special Events Society Certification Committee, Suzanne Bristow, CSEP; Tiffany Danley, CSEP, CMP; Lisa Delpy, Ph.D.; Klaus Inkamp, CSEP; Robert Sivek, CSEP; Ralph Traxler, CSEP; and Susan Weston, Ed.D., have provided the leadership and expertise to ensure that this project reached fruition. Additionally, many members of The International Special Events Society (ISES), most notably Dana Zita, CSEP, of Toronto, Canada, and Lena Malouf of Sydney, Australia, provided important feedback to offer further validation. R. Robert Graves, Sharon Moore, and members of the Greater Delaware ISES Chapter provided significant early direction to ensure the format is easy to read and the information is useful to event managers.

The editors extend their gratitude to the following Master's degree students in Tourism with a concentration in Event Management at The George Washington University. They have touched these terms with a fresh vitality that is an inspiration to every event management professional. Our industry's future is secure due to the talent, generosity, and persistence of these event management scholars.

Original Editorial Team
Mary Toups
Guion Williams
Jennifer Ziehl

Final Editorial Team
Karen Baker
Erin McGee

Acknowledgments

Event Management Graduate Students

Ayhan Bayer, Janna Bowman, Rob Caskey, Kimberly Collins, Arnold Ehrlich, Andrea Frank, Amy Galton, Michelle Glemser, Tanya Headley, Dana Jarvis, Bill Knight, Laurie Lowe, Stephen Masten, Sara May, Cynthia McDowell, Terrance Morris, Kari Nestande, Gabriel Ornelas, Kristan Quackenbush, Lisa Shafran, Kathy Siegfried, Traci Silke-Punke, Annie Stine, Arden Tellini, Tamera Thomason, Darnyce Werth, Anita Wiler, Nancy Yim, and Suk Kyu Yoon

Disclaimer

A reasonable effort has been made by the editors and contributors to validate the terms in this book. However, the editors, the International Special Events Society, or the publisher are not responsible for errors and omissions. The editors invite the readers of this first *Dictionary of Event Management* to further contribute to the expansion and dissemination of knowledge in the Event Management profession with recommendations for additions or corrections in future editions of this book. Please send your comments to:

Editorial Board
Dictionary of Event Management
The Event Management Program
The George Washington University
2100 Pennsylvania Avenue NW Suite 250
Washington, DC 20037
or via facsimile to
(202) 223-1387
or via electronic mail to
drevent@gwis2.circ.gwu.edu

A-440 The designated international pitch to which pianos are tuned.

AAF See **American Academy of Florists.**

abstract 1. A written summary of a speech or paper, generally between 200-500 words; see **Summary/Brief** or **Call for Papers.** 2. In laser presentations, graphic designs or patterns that are not representational of concrete objects; often waveform or lissajous patterns, which are *abstract* electronic patterns that appear organic in view. 3. Brief statement of content.

accompanying person A person who attends an event with a *participant*; see **significant other** or **spouse.**

account codes A number system given to specific categories of income or expense; see **code of accounts.**

account executive A person who represents the company and the client in servicing both in a business arrangement.

ACEDI See **Association of Conference and Event Directors International.**

accreditation 1. An official recognition or authorization by an independent accrediting organization. 2. The process required for receiving **credentials** for access to an event or a certain area of an event.

Acousto-Optico Modulation A technique for chopping or colorizing laser images in which primary laser color (red, green, blue) passes through an acousto-optical (AO) crystal, electrically modulated to transmit color. These beams converge into a single beam that proceeds to the XY scanners and the projection surface.

Act of God An accident or event resulting from natural causes, that is not preventable by reasonable foresight or care; i.e., flood, hurricane, earthquake, and war; see **force majeure clause.**

Actors' Equity (AE) A professional union that represents performers, stage managers, and others who appear in live theater.

ACTRA See **Association of Cable Television and Radio Artists.**

actuator A solenoid-type device, usually 2-position, used in laser light shows, activated by an electric closure, which is sometimes used for shutters, as well as beam-positioning.

AD See **assistant director**.

ADA See **Americans with Disabilities Act**.

adjoining room A room sharing a common wall with another room but without a connecting door.

additional insured An individual or organization listed as covered by a primary insurance agreement.

advance order A good or service ordered before **move-in** date.

advance registration An enrollment to an event made prior to opening day.

advancing colors The colors found on the left side of the standard color wheel, such as red, orange, and yellow.

advertised air tour A published, planned travel program with assigned **inclusive tour** number usually at a special air fare and requiring pre-payment.

advertising A message that media (newspaper, magazine, television, for example) is paid to distribute. The **sponsor** controls the message.

AE See **Actor's Equity** and **Account Executive**.

aerial beams See **atmospheric**.

AFTA See **Australian Federation of Travel Agents**.

AFTRA See **American Federation of Television and Radio Artists**.

agenda A written schedule of an event, providing pertinent information, including time, sequence of topics and sessions, location, and presenters' names.

agent 1. A person empowered to act on the behalf of entertainers, speakers or other contracted agents, for a fee, and who has no

à la russe

legal or financial responsibility other than for areas of professional liability resulting from those acts.

AGVA   See **American Guild of Variety Artists.**

AHMA   See **American Hotel and Motel Association.**

AIA   See **Australian Incentive Association.**

AIFD   See **American Institute of Floral Designers.**

AIM   See **Australian Institute of Management.**

air-cooled laser   A high-intensity lamp creating laser-like beams operating on a standard 115 VAC, cooled by air; used for indoor presentations, primarily safe for an audience scan effect.

air space   The space between air walls that separates event rooms to create better sound.

Air Transport Association of America (ATAA)   An organization for members who are concerned with airlines' operation.

Air Traffic Conference of America (ATC)   Division of *Air Transport Association* (**ATA**) that establishes industry standards and methods of operation.

air walls   A movable, sound-resistant barrier that partitions event areas; also known as **movable wall, partition** or **divider.**

aisle   A passageway between rows of tables, chairs, booths, or stands, the width determined by local fire regulations; also known as **Bridgeway** or **Gangway.**

aisle carpet   A floor covering installed in passageways.

aisle sign   A posting of aisle numbers or letters, indicating locations of participant **booths** or **stands.**

à la carte (a la kart)   A menu with a separate price for each item as opposed to a fixed price for an entire meal.

à la russe (a la rOOs)   A method of food service in which each guest is served a plate completely set up.

A

all risk coverage Property insurance covering losses arising from any fortuitous cause except those that are specifically excluded.

all space hold A term which indicates all facility space that is reserved for one client.

alterations A production change made by the client after work has begun, and may be billed as extra charges.

ambient light A level of illumination used to create a particular atmosphere using existing or additional lighting sources.

amenity 1. A complimentary item provided by facility management and found in sleeping rooms, i.e., writing supplies, bathrobe, fruit basket, shower cap, shampoo, shoe shine mitt. 2. A complimentary service product provided by a **host** or **sponsor** of an event for the purposes of advertising and good will; also known as **giveaways.**

America Online (AOL) A major electronic messaging and on-line service connected to the **Internet.**

American breakfast A hotel term to designate a morning meal which consists of cereal, eggs, meat, bakery goods, fruits, juices, and beverages; also known as **Full Breakfast.**

American Academy of Florists (AAF) A school based in Chicago, IL that trains persons in floral design.

American Federation of Television and Radio Artists (AFTRA) A labor union that represents performers on audiotape, radio, television, and videotape.

American Guild of Variety Artists (AGVA) A labor union that represents performers who appear in nightclubs, circuses, touring attractions, and other special events.

American Hotel and Motel Association (AHMA) An organization whose members work in hotels and motels and provide service and products for the hotel and motel industry.

American Institute of Floral Designers (AIFD) An international organization that provides seminars and workshops to professional florists who display their designs in shows and events.

animation (slides)

American Plan An overnight room accommodation which includes breakfast, lunch, and dinner; also known as **Full American Plan (FAP).**

Americans with Disabilities Act (ADA) U.S. legislation passed in 1992 requiring public buildings (offices, hotels, restaurants, etc.) to make adjustments meeting minimum standards to make their facilities accessible for individuals with physical disabilities.

American Society for Training and Development (ASTD) A large organization whose members are training specialists and those who provide services for the training industry, offering a myriad of educational opportunities and materials for its members.

American Society of Association Executives (ASAE) An organization providing information, resources, and education to its members who are trade association executives and those who provide services and products for the association industry.

American Society of Travel Agents (ASTA) An organization of travel agents throughout the world, whose members provide travel services and products; provides information, resources, and education to its members.

amp 1. Ampere, a standard unit measuring the strength of an electrical current. 2. Amplifier; also known as **power amplifier.**

amplifier An electronic device that drives speakers in audio systems.

anamorphic lens A lens adapter designed to produce a wide screen image.

anchor An auger-type device used to secure the **guy ropes** of a tent to the ground, ranging in length from 30" to 48" with a helix of 4" to 8" in diameter. Anchors hold better than stakes do in bare earth and sand; also known as **Stakes.**

animation (slides) 1. A technique that creates an illusion of movement when used in rapid sequence; see **cel animation, computer animation, slide animation.**

antitrust laws U.S. legislation designed to promote competition and prevent unfair practices that may lead to monopolies or suppression of competition.

AOL See **America Online.**

aperture width/height The dimensions of a slide or film frame.

apex fare Advance Purchase Excursion Fare (airline). Special fare at a lower rate.

apron The part of a stage in front of the main curtain.

Archie A service on the **Internet** for gathering, indexing, and displaying information (such as a list of the files available through anonymous file retrieval and transfer services).

arc light A now outdated light source providing high intensity light utilizing a positive and negative metal rod (instead of a light bulb) for large screens or long projection distances; also used in follow spot lights. Replaced by **xenon lamps** in the 1980s.

argon An inert, colorless, odorless gas that creates a blue-green color inside a laser tube.

arrangement background Determines the shape—height, width, and breadth.

arrangement focal point The center or heart of a floral design.

arrival pattern The anticipated dates and times of arrival of group members.

arrival time The anticipated time guests are expected to arrive at a facility.

art Any materials (drawings, photographs, type) used in preparing camera-ready art; also known as artwork.

art principles An accepted principle encompassing line, form, color, texture, and pattern.

ASAE See **American Society of Association Executives.**

atmospheric

ash can See **ash stand.**

ash stand A receptacle for tobacco ashes; ashtray.

ASM See **assistant stage manager.**

aspect ratio The ratio of image width to height; pertaining to audio-visual, video, and slides.

assistant director (AD) A person who assists the director in supervising other workers; also known as an **associate director.**

assistant stage manager (ASM) A person who assists the **Stage Manager** by taking responsibility for the stage area only.

associate director See **assistant director.**

assembly A general or formal meeting of an organization for the purpose of deciding legislative direction, approving policy, electing committee members, approving balance sheets, budgets, etc. Rules of procedure as prescribed in an organization's Articles & By-laws are observed.

Association of Cable Television and Radio Artists (ACTRA) An organization for artists who perform on audiotape, radio, and cable television.

Association of Conference and Event Directors International (ACEDI) An organization whose members work in colleges and universities as conference and event managers.

ASTA See **American Society of Travel Agents.**

ASTD See **American Society for Training and Development.**

AT&T Mail A major mail and on-line system connected to the **Internet.**

athletic event An event that involves athletes in competition or demonstration.

atmospheric A term used to describe a lighting effect created by laser light projected through the air, often enhanced with theatrical fog; also known as **aerial beams.**

ATAA See **Air Transport Association of America.**

ATC See **Air Traffic Conference of America.**

attendance The total number of people attending an event.

attendee An individual person attending an event.

attender An individual person attending event sessions, although not officially involved with the event; also known as an observer.

audience left or right The stage direction as seen from the audience perspective; see **camera left,** and **right; screen** and **audience left and right; stage left, stage right.**

audioconference A conference using only voice transmissions between two or more sites.

audio monitor A speaker used for listening to the playback of tapes or records and by musicians to hear themselves or other musicians on stage.

audiovisual Designates equipment, materials, and teaching aids used in sound and visual presentations.

audit 1. A certified count of attendance. 2. Official review of finances by a Certified Public Accountant.

auditorium lens A projection lens used for long distances.

auditorium setup An arrangement of chairs in rows facing a head table, stage, or speaker; the rows may be straight or semicircular; also known as a church seating or **theater setup;** see **V-shaped setup.**

Australian Federation of Travel Agents (AFTA) An organization whose members work as travel agents and are from Australia or service Australia.

Australian Institute of Management (AIM) A school in Australia that specializes in international business management.

awards banquet/celebration

authorized signature A signature of a person(s) with the authority to: (1) charge to an organization's master account; (2) guarantee payment; and/or (3) contract for space, services, and supplies; also known as **signatory.**

author's guideline/kit The instructions regarding the required format for the written presentation of a speech; also known as **preparation of paper.**

automatic advance A feature on a slide projector that mechanically inserts the next slide.

automobile liability insurance An insurance coverage which protects the owner/operator of the motor vehicle from financial risk due to accidents caused by the driver; also known as **third party policy.**

AV contractor A supplier of audio-visual equipment, including projectors, screens, sound systems, video, staging, and technical staff.

awards banquet/celebration An event, usually formal, to honor outstanding performance.

B

bale ring

B&B See **bed and breakfast.**

B lights A string of 35 to 100 half-watt miniature lights spaced 8" apart; also known as mini-Italian, bud, or fairy lights.

back curtain Swagged tent curtains, approximately 30" wide, used for decorative purposes on side poles.

back-to-back A travel program operating on a continuous basis so that as one group arrives another soon departs.

back-to-base Communication means for event staff and security officers to contact headquarters.

backdrop A drape, curtain, or fabric panel at the back of a stage, speaker's table, or exhibit booth.

back projection The process by which an image is projected on the back of a stage or screen which is placed between the viewer and the projector or R.P.; also known as **rear screen projection.**

backline equipment Rented equipment required by performers such as amplifiers, microphones, or other items.

backstage The portion of the stage behind the main curtain, including the stage, dressing rooms, and wings.

backup facilities Substitute event space that is booked as part of the planning strategy and used should planned space be insufficient.

backwall booth An exhibitor's booth which is located on the perimeter or rear wall and not considered premier booth space.

badge Identification worn by event participants; also known as a **name tag.**

baffle Partition to control light, air, sound, or traffic flow.

bale ring A means of raising tents by raising center poles and securing them with **guy ropes.** The peak at the center poles is secured to a bale ring (a metal ring), which in turn is raised (along with the roof of the tent) by block and tackle to its ultimate or ideal height on the center poles.

ball A formal social dance.

banjo (fabric) A type of lightweight cloth used for **backdrops;** also known as **calico.**

bank draft A written authorization by an individual or agency for the transfer of money into another account; a check.

bank remittance A deposit forwarded to a bank by mail, personal, or electronic means.

bank transfer A movement of funds from one bank account to another.

banner A suspended rectangular piece of fabric or paper used for decorations or signs.

banquet A formal or ceremonial dinner held during an event, including speeches, music, etc.

banquet captain The person responsible for all food service; for larger functions may be responsible for a specific area of the dining room; also known as **captain, supervisor,** or **maitre d'.**

banquet check A check or bill issued to a client for food and beverage orders for an event based on the **banquet event order.**

banquet event order (BEO) A form providing detailed instructions prepared by an event facility; provides details such as food and beverage, and room setup to facility personnel concerned with a specific area of the function dining room. Also known as resumé, function sheet, event order, **running order/schedule.**

banquet round A circular table used for meal service; depending on the diameter, can comfortably seat up to 12 people.

barn doors Movable, hinged flaps used to control intensity of stage lights.

bar-mitzvah A Jewish religious ceremony on a male's thirteenth birthday marking the entry into maturity and often accompanied by social celebration.

bar reading A detailed written record of liquor consumption during an event.

barrier-free Absence of obstacles preventing handicapped persons from moving freely to all public areas.

base A steel floor support piece designed to support an upright post.

basic elements Accepted elements that encompass dominance, scale, rhythm, harmony, and space.

bas/bat-mitzvah A Jewish religious ceremony on the thirteenth birthday of a female, marking her entry into adulthood and often accompanied by social celebrations.

batten (Bats) A lengths of pipe from which scenery, curtains, and lights can be hung; also known as **timber battens.**

BBS See **bulletin board system.**

beaded-screen See **glass-beaded screen.**

beams, or beam sculptures A designed array of high-power laser beams, which can be sent directly from the laser source into infinity or bounced off carefully aligned mirrors to create complex compositions. Beam sculptures can be static or kinetic; if kinetic, they can be sequenced through reconfigured positions or scanned (swept) across space; also known as **mirrors.**

bed and breakfast (B&B) A room rate that includes a sleeping room and breakfast often in homes or inns and in small intimate locations; also known as **continental plan (CP).**

beep An audio signal used in cueing and editing.

b/g Background, as in background music.

bell captain A hotel employee who supervises the work of the bell staff.

bell staff Hotel personnel charged with escorting guests to rooms, carrying luggage, and running errands.

BEO See **banquet event order.**

beta See **VHS**.

bid document A proposal submitted by a destination or a venue inviting a group to meet in their venue.

bid manual/specifications A written document sent to vendors and issued by an organization that contains requirements for their future events that outlines primary selection and decision procedures; also known as **request for proposal (RFP)** or **job tender**.

bill of lading A document or form listing goods to be shipped.

Bitnet (BIT-net) A network of mostly IBM main frames connected to the **Internet**.

BIX A commercial system on the **Internet** formerly run by *Byte* magazine and now run by General Videotext.

black powder A chemical mixture of potassium nitrate, sulfur, and charcoal used as the propellant for fireworks shells.

black tie A term which requires a tuxedo or dinner jacket, bow tie, and cummerbund for men and formal evening dress for women; in the U.S. and Canada, **black tie** indicates tuxedo; also known as **formal dress** and **national dress**.

black tie optional A term which indicates formal dress, i.e., tuxedo, evening dress, is preferred but not required.

blackboard A hard, smooth, dark surface for drawing or writing with chalk; also known as **chalkboard.**

blanking A momentary diversion of laser light into a light trap within the laser optics, creating a discontinuity, or black space, within the laser graphic which may be fast, slow, clean, wiped, accurate, or approximate, depending on the equipment.

bleachers A tiered seating space, usually without cover, for spectators of events; also known as **grandstand.**

bleed A printing term in which ink runs to the edge of the paper.

blending of color A gradual merging of one color into another.

block Number of rooms held for a group for a specified period of time.

block and tackle Ropes and pulleys used to lift and to pull out stress points where greater leverage is required; for example, used to lift and stretch tents.

blocked space A term which indicates that sleeping rooms, exhibit, meeting, or other function space has been reserved by an organization holding a future event.

blocking A rehearsal, during which the director sets up all the action or movements for the scene.

bloom 1. A flower or blossom of a plant. 2. A powdery substance seen on the surface of freshly picked fruit.

blow up An enlargement of a photo, a piece of art, or typography.

blueline\blueprint A final proof copy for client's approval before printing; also known as **brownline, silverprint,** or **proof.**

board meeting A meeting of the governing body of an organization.

board of director's setup A configuration of tables in a meeting room set in a rectangular or oval shape with chairs placed on both sides of the tables and at the ends; also known as a **conference-style setup** or **board room setup.**

board room A meeting room set up permanently with a table and suitable seating.

board room setup A configuration of tables set in a rectangular or oval shape with chairs placed on both sides and at the ends; also known as **conference-style setup** or **board of director's setup.**

boarding pass A permit to board a ship, train, plane, or other form of transportation.

body type The type size used for main text.

boldface In printing, a type with a heavy face.

bonded warehouse

bonded warehouse A warehouse authorized by customs authorities for storage of goods on which payment of duties is deferred until the goods are removed.

bone yard An equipment storage area at an event site.

bonus See **perquisite** or **gratuity**.

book To commit ahead of time meeting-room space, sleeping rooms, speakers, or entertainers on a definite basis.

book of abstracts A collection of **abstracts** available to meeting participants for use in selecting sessions.

book-on-payment (BOP) A payment guaranteed by a travel agency for a package reserved within a cancellation period.

boom arm An adjustable support for positioning microphones, lighting fixtures, or video cameras.

boom microphone A microphone attached to a long, movable arm and used in stage production.

booth A specific area assigned by management to an exhibitor under contractual agreement; also known as **stand.**

booth number A number designation to identify each exhibitor's space.

booth personnel The staff assigned to represent the exhibitor in an assigned space.

booth sign 1. An identification stating name, city, state, and booth number of exhibitor. 2. Sign behind desk indicating service provided at that point; also known as **fascia board.**

booth size The dimensions of an exhibitor's space.

booth/stand area The amount of floor space occupied by an exhibitor.

booth/stand contractor A company which constructs or assembles exhibit booths/stands under contract with the organizing committee.

border chaser   Programmed lighting around signs.

boundary microphone   See **plate microphone** or **PZM**.

box lunch   A light lunch in a box.

brainstorming   A group technique for stimulating creative ideas which are not initially judged for merit.

break   A short interval between sessions when coffee, tea, and other refreshments are served; also known as **coffee break,** or **refreshment break.**

breakdown   The time required to dismantle the structure of an event.

breakup   An image or audio distortion.

breakout sessions   Small groups formed within a meeting to discuss topics related to the general session.

bridgeway   See **aisle** and **gangway**.

brief   See **summary brief.**

brilliance   The degree of intensity of colors.

Bring Your Own (BYO)   A term which refers to the practice of bringing alcoholic beverages to restaurants and establishments which charge a **corkage** fee for that privilege.

broadcast equipment   High-caliber video equipment used by television stations, production companies and other broadcasting professionals who require a quality visual product.

brochure   A pamphlet describing and promoting a particular event or product.

brownline   See **blueline.**

Brussels Tariff Nomenclature   The customs tariff used by many countries, including most European nations, but not the U.S.; also known as Customs Cooperation Council, Nomenclature of, or **custom duties.**

budget A financial statement of estimated income and expenditure for a specific time period. See **budget chart, cash flow chart, phased budget.**

budget chart The estimated total revenue and expenditure, divided into subject categories projecting cash needed to meet expenses over specific time frame; also known as **cash flow chart, phased budget,** or **budget.**

buffer zone (Canadian) The zone in Canada, 225 miles from the border, dividing the two tax structures applied to Y class fares.

buffer zone (PRS) A section of seats on a plane located between smoking and non-smoking sections allowing for variance in the smoking and non-smoking boundary.

buffet An assortment of foods offered on a table and self-served.

build The process of adding lines or changes to a series of sequential slides; also known as multiple disclosure.

bulkhead The seats at the front of an airplane cabin facing a wall.

bullet A large, heavy dot used in printing for emphasis or enumeration.

bullet hit A pyrotechnic device used to simulate the effects (visual or audio) of a rifle or gun shot.

Bulletin Board System (BBS) A computer system used by various special interest and discussion groups to communicate electronically on an on-going basis.

bump-in See **move-in.**

bumping The process of removing a confirmed airline passenger from a full flight to make room for a passenger with higher priority.

bump-out See **move-out.**

bunting 1. Linen gathered together in loose folds on top of a table and suitable seating. 2. Flags, banners, or swagged strips of cloth hung as festive decorations.

buzz session

burn units See **smoke generation.**

bus 1. A motor-driven vehicle for transporting groups of people. 2. Generally refers to the physical connection used on the "motherboards" or "backplanes" within an electronic equipment enclosure, such as a personal computer, to cross connect two or more circuit boards so that electronically coded messages can pass back and forth between the individual components that make up the overall system. May either take the form of a multiconductor cable with connectors attached or a printed circuit board with edge connectors to accommodate plugging in other circuit boards.

business attire Business suits or jackets with shirts and ties for men and day dresses or suits for women; usually taken to mean office and not recreational wear; can include informal forms of **national dress;** also known as **informal dress.**

business manager A person responsible for the finances and elements of the production for the client and for the public.

business center An area in hotel or meeting facility offering office equipment and services; see **communication center.**

business class An airline service priced between first and economy class and offering special amenities.

business occurring A phrase referring to the number of groups and attendees meeting in a city during a specific time frame.

busy A cluttered image on the screen.

butler service (American) A method of serving in which waiters move amongst the guests serving food and drinks; also known as **tray service** in Australia.

butler service (Australia) A personalized method of serving in which the waiter holds a platter as the guests serve themselves; also known as **formal dining service.**

buzz session A method used to increase participation by dividing participants into smaller discussion groups which then report their findings and opinions in plenary session.

by the bottle

by the bottle Liquor served and charged for by the full bottle.

by the drink Liquor served and charged for by the number of drinks served.

by the piece Food purchased by the individual piece, usually for a reception.

by the person A fixed price that covers food consumption within a given time frame; sometimes includes snacks or hors d'oeurves or canapés.

BYO See **Bring Your Own.**

cancellation clause

cabana (ka-BAN-ya) A room adjacent to pool area, with or without sleeping facilities.

cabaret table A small round table, 15" to 30" in diameter, used for cocktail parties; also known as a **club table, cocktail table, cocktail round,** or in Australia as **le cafe table** in off-premise catering.

CAEM See **Canadian Association of Exposition Managers.**

calico See **banjo.**

call board A theater bulletin board for announcements of rehearsals, work calls, and general theater information.

call brand A specific brand of liquor selected by a client according to personal preference for serving at an event; see **house brand.**

call for papers A document containing detailed instructions for the submission of papers which are assessed and selected by a review committee; often referred to as *abstract* forms; also known as **abstract** and **conference papers.**

camera chain Television cameras, cables, video controls, and power supply working together.

camera left and right The direction from the camera's (or audience's) perspective, as opposed to from the stage, or performer's perspective.

camera-ready art Materials ready for photographic reproduction.

Canadian Association of Exposition Managers (CAEM) An organization providing information and resources to its members who work for hotels or convention centers as exposition managers.

Canadian Hotel and Motel Association (CHMA) A Canadian organization providing information, education, and resources to its members who work in hotel and motel operations.

cancellation clause 1. A contract provision that outlines penalties for both parties for cancellation or failure to comply with terms of the agreement. 2. A contract provision in the entertainment

cancellation insurance

industry which allows an artist to cancel a performance within a specified time prior to play date.

cancellation insurance A policy that protects the financial interests of the event sponsor or event organizer in the event of a cancellation.

candelabra An ornamental, branched candlestick.

canopy A drapery, awning, or other roof-like covering which provides overhanging shelter.

canvas A heavy cloth used for outdoor banners, tents, and sails. Vinyl is commonly used in Australia.

capacity A maximum number of people who can be contained in any given area.

capacity control A restriction on the number of seats available for a particular fare or event.

captain The person responsible for food-related services at banquet functions; also known as **banquet captain.**

cardioid microphone (KAR-di-oid) A unidirectional microphone often used on lecterns that picks up sound in a heart-shaped pattern; see **lectern microphone.**

Carnet (KAR-ne) A customs document which permits its holder to carry or send merchandise into a designated foreign country for a defined period of time for the purpose of display or demonstration without paying customs fees or posting bonds.

carousel projector The Eastman Kodak brand name for a 35mm slide projector using a carousel tray.

carousel tray A circular holder used for projecting 35mm slides; also known as **round slidetray.**

carpenter A person skilled in the building and repair of wooden objects and used for fabrication and installation of booths, stands, exhibits, and environmental designs.

ceiling decor

carrier A company employed to transport passengers or freight. Uses all or some space on an airplane, bus, ship, or other vehicle during a special period of time and for a specific itinerary.

cartage Short-haul moving of exhibits; often incorrectly referred to as drayage; also known as **transport** or **freight**.

CASE See **Council for the Advancement and Support of Education.**

cash bar A private bar set up where guests pay for drinks.

cash flow chart Same as **budget chart, phased budget, budget.**

cash registration The full payment of estimated room charges at time of hotel guest registration; credit for incidentals, such as room and laundry services, and telephone charges, are not extended.

cash reservation A payment made at time of reservation for anticipated charges.

cassette A self-enclosed two-reel tape module, audio, or video.

casual attire A term used to designate a sports shirt, possibly with a jacket, for men and dressy casual wear, such as slack outfits, fashionable casual dresses, or resort-type outfits for women.

catering sales manager The hotel or facility staff person responsible for servicing group and local food and beverage functions; staff person responsible for selling property to potential clients.

catenary arch The curve made by a flexible, nonelastic chain or cord when it is suspended freely between two points of the same height as referring to tents.

catwalk A narrow walkway above an auditorium used for hanging lights and sound equipment.

CD See **compact disk.**

CDRH See **Center for Devices and Radiological Health.**

ceiling decor Suspended decorations to enhance appearances of venue.

ceiling height

ceiling height Maximum height of ceiling of a venue. Dimensions quoted by halls and hotels often do not take into account any light fixtures hanging from the ceiling or lowest ceiling points.

CEIR See **Center for Exhibition Industry Research.**

cel animation A succession of rapidly changing drawings, or cels, which create the sense of movement, as in film; see **animation (slides).**

celebrate To observe with ceremony and ritual.

Center for Devices and Radiological Health (CDRH) A division of the U.S. Food and Drug Administration that regulates the use of lasers in the United States, including those used for display purposes.

Center for Exhibition Industry Research (CEIR) An organization that conducts research for the trade show industry for the purpose of determining economic impact and other market research.

center poles Solid or telescopic poles of wood or metal used to support the center and highest part of a tent.

center sections The sections of a tent that form the roof between the two end sections.

centerpiece A decorative object placed at the center of a banquet table.

CEO See **Chief Executive Officer.**

Certificate of Origin An official government document stating origin of foreign goods.

Certificate of Insurance Serves as written evidence of insurance.

Certificate of Insurance Currency A document proving an organization has public liability insurance.

Certified Meeting Professional (CMP) A designation offered by the **Convention Liaison Council (CLC)** that certifies competency in twenty-five areas of meeting management.

Certified Special Events Professional (CSEP) A designation signifying the hallmark of professional achievement in event management, administered by the **International Special Events Society (ISES).**

CEUs See **Continuing Education Units.**

CFO See **Chief Financial Officer.**

chain lock A security device that limits the opening of a door by a chain that can be attached to the door jamb.

chair person A person selected to preside over a session, meeting, committee, board, or conference.

chalkboard See **blackboard.**

change order A facility form used to advise departments of changes in reservations or functions.

charter The exclusive use of all or some space on an airplane, bus, ship, or other vehicle for a special period of time and fare and for a specific itinerary.

charts Music books, sheets, or scores.

character generator An electronic device which displays words or characters within a television image.

chaser A mild drink that is consumed following hard liquor.

chaser lights A system of lights wired so that a mechanical or computerized device can control different lights and their pattern (forward, reverse, alternating, random, or cascade).

chaser music See **walk in/out music.**

cheat To vary the positions of actors to create a better television or stage picture.

Council of Engineering & Scientific Society Executives (CESSE) An organization providing education, information, and resources for engineering and science professionals who work for societies in an administrative, legislative, or advisory position.

check-in A registration procedure for guests at the time of arrival.

check-in time The time at which a guest may check in and occupy rooms.

check-out

check-out   A procedure at the time of guest departure, including account settlement.

check-out time   The time set by a facility when guests are required to vacate rooms.

chef's choice   The selection of food items by the chef which best complement the entree or main course and which can demonstrate the chef's culinary ability.

cherry picker   A piece of heavy equipment used to lift a person to a given height; also known as **high jacker**.

chevron   1. A type of room set up with chairs and/or tables arranged in a "V" shaped pattern; also known as **herringbone setup** or **V-shaped setup**. 2. Type of cloth used for **backdrops**.

Chief Executive Officer (CEO)   The principal officer responsible for the overall administration of an organization.

Chief Financial Officer (CFO)   The individual in an organization responsible for the financial management of the company.

Chief Operating Officer (COO)   The executive responsible for day-to-day operations of an organization.

Chinagraph pen/pencil   A special pen/pencil used for marking on print overlays and acetates because it rubs off easily.

CHMA   See **Canadian Hotel and Motel Association**.

civic celebration   An event that celebrates civic pride through parades, festivals, and other annual traditional programs.

chopping   In laser presentations, a form of **blanking** that is not often used to create discretionary blank spaces (such as spaces between letters in a word), but, is used to lace abstract graphics with a wave-form pattern of black, to create an attractive interference pattern.

classroom seating   See **schoolroom setup**.

classroom setup   A configuration of tables set in rows, one behind the other, with chairs facing the stage; also known as **schoolroom setup**.

coach

CLC See **Convention Liaison Council.**

clear-span tents Tents with an aluminum frame support structure that eliminate the need for center pole support.

clinic/workshop A hands-on educational experience where students learn or improve skills by doing.

clearance 1. Permission obtained to use restricted property. 2. The space between a passing object or the roof of a passageway.

clogged head The accumulation of oxide on the head of a videocassette recorder which results in noise, breakup, or loss of picture.

close-up A picture composition in which only a small portion of the person, place, or thing being filmed, photographed, televised, or videotaped fills the frame.

closed/fully booked See **full house.**

closed-end The number of incentive/travel winners—limited by a predetermined amount.

closing ceremony The final activities at an event that occur during the **closing session.**

closing session The final gathering of an event in which the meeting topics are summarized and conclusions are announced.

club manager A specialist who manages events, food and beverage, and business activities for a club.

club table See **cabaret table.**

cluster 1. Enclosed lights used to illuminate the top of film and stage sets. 2. A group of speakers mounted in auditoriums, arenas, and theaters.

CMP See **Certified Meeting Professional.**

CNYT See **Current New York Time.**

coach A trainer or instructor who develops special skills, i.e., public presentation.

coach fare

coach fare   Economy fare.

coated stock   Paper manufactured with coatings of clay or other materials to give the base paper a smooth, often glossy, surface.

coaxial cable   1. Cable used to carry audio and television signals. 2. A type of transmission line, used for high-frequency television, telegraph, and telephone signals.

cocktail table/cocktail round   See **cabaret table**.

code of accounts   See **account codes**.

coffee break   See **refreshment break** or **break**.

coherent light   Light waves that stay almost parallel and are in sync with each other, working together to produce a concentrated and very bright beam like that of a laser.

co-insured   Legally no such term exists, but informally it represents an additional insured.

cold call   A sales call made without an appointment.

colloquium/academic conference or seminar   An informal participatory discussion, usually of an academic or research nature, used to identify areas of mutual interest through the exchange of ideas and held irregularly.

collimator   (kol-LIM-a-tor) A device that makes rays of light more parallel; used to reduce the divergence of laser light for very long throws (long length light must reach from origin to destination) and at the output of transmission fibers.

color key proof   A medium to view color images and copy.

color wheel   A motorized, revolving metal disk, approximately 18" in diameter, with five or six holes cut around the perimeter, each covered with a color filter, and mounted to a light source. As the disk rotates, the filters pass through the light beam creating a changing pattern of color.

combo   A small jazz or dance band.

comet In pyrotechnics, a star formation that is round (the size of a quarter and manufactured in the Far East) or square (the size of a pool chalk and manufactured in Italy). A large pellet of powder, either round or cylindrical, ignites, propels the star, and leaves a comet-like tail.

commencement/graduation The event that celebrates graduation from the highest grade in a particular school or college.

commercial general liability A broad form of liability insurance providing protection from liability claims for bodily injury and property damage resulting from the use of products or services, or completed operations, excluding automobile liability.

commercial invoice A document specifying content of a shipment of goods.

commercial rate See **corporate rate.**

commissionable A type of sale in which a fee, or percentage of the amount of sale, is to be paid to the agent or purchaser.

commitment An agreement between client and facility to reserve function and guest room space; also known as **contract** or **letter of agreement.**

commitment ritual The religious or spiritual event wherein two individuals proclaim their life-long commitment to one another. Popular in alternative lifestyles such as gay and lesbian.

committee A group of people elected or appointed to perform specific functions.

common carrier A transportation company which handles crated or any materials.

communication center/business center An area in event venue for telephone, fax, telex, teleconferencing facilities, and other business equipment.

commuter airline An air service providing connecting flights between small communities and larger airports.

comp An abbreviation for **complimentary.**

comp rooms Complimentary room(s) which a facility provides without charge based on the number of paid rooms occupied by a group.

compact disk A circular device which stores large amounts of information, including music, video, and electronic data as in a *CD-ROM.* See **CD**.

compere (kom-PARE) See **MC**.

complete meeting package An all-inclusive plan offered by conference centers.

complimentary Service, space, or item offered without charge; see **comp**.

complimentary registration A service provided where the fee has been waived.

comprehensive general (public) liability insurance An umbrella insurance policy that the Event Manager or event sponsor must maintain in full force to cover injuries, fire, theft, and other potential liabilities; covers lawsuits brought forth by event participants.

comprehensive layout An artist's precise rendering of proposed piece showing paper and color selection, size and placement of type, illustrations and photographs.

CompuServe A large on-line service on the **Internet.**

computer animation The creation and/or manipulation of moving artwork with a computer program; see **animation (slides)**.

computer card (registration) See **registration card key**.

computerized registration Automated registration records.

Conceptual Art An artist's impression/drawing of a proposed event.

concert rider See **rider**.

concessions The sale of promotional items, such as albums, posters, T-shirts, by artist's representatives; usually set up in conjunction with artist's engagement.

concierge 1. A facility staff person who arranges information and services to guests including tickets, transportation, and tour arrangements. 2. Designated area in facility providing special amenities and services to guests.

concurrent sessions Event meetings which are held during the same time period.

conclave A private meeting or assembly for a group with shared or special interests.

condensed type A narrow or slender type that permits a greater number of characters per line.

condenser microphone Microphone with an electronically charged element which allows a fuller frequency response but is a more delicate device; used to amplify piano or string music and soprano singers; also known as **Electret**.

cone A pencil-thin laser beam that is scanned very quickly, in a circle, to which fog is introduced, producing a solid cone of light; also a part of the sound speaker.

conference 1. Participatory meeting designed for discussion of subjects related to a specific topic or area. May include fact finding, problem solving, and consultation. 2. An event used by any organization to meet and exchange views, convey a message, open a debate, or give publicity to some area of opinion on a specific issue. No tradition, continuity, or specific period is required to convene a conference. Although not generally limited in time, conferences are usually of short duration with specific objectives. Conferences are generally on a smaller scale than congresses and/or conventions. 3. Assembly of large number of individuals to discuss items of mutual interest or engage in professional development through learning.

conference handbook

conference handbook A manual which provides information about a conference, including the schedule of events, the agenda, the description of programs, information on participants, and logistical information.

conference officer/organizer A title conferred upon the chief administrator of the entire event; see **Professional Congress Organizer (PCO)**.

conference pack/kit A comprehensive collection of conference documentation within a binder or envelope; also known as information kit or **registration packet**.

conference papers A collection of abstracts of lectures to be presented during a conference compiled in the book of abstracts; see **call for papers**.

conference report An official summary of conference events.

conference-style setup A configuration of tables set in a rectangular or oval shape with chairs placed on both sides, and at the ends of the tables; see **board of directors setup**.

configuration 1. Arrangement of seats within an aircraft. 2. Sleeping berth in a day/night compartment on a European train.

confirmation A written acknowledgment of a reservation request.

confirmed reservation An oral or written agreement to provide accommodations on a particular date, rate, and type for a specified number of guests; oral agreement may require a credit card number to guarantee availability.

congress 1. A scheduled, periodic meeting of delegates or representatives of interested groups to discuss some subject. 2. The European term for convention.

congress travel agent A travel agent specializing in handling incoming or outgoing meeting participants and all their future travel arrangements including pre- and post-tours.

connecting canopy An awning between two tents that provides a protected passageway.

continental buffet

connecting rooms Two or more adjoined rooms with private connecting doors.

consecutive interpretation The oral translation of conversation or speeches from one language to another as the speaker pauses between phrases to allow for interpretation; also known as **simultaneous interpretation.**

consignee The person or agency to whom goods are shipped.

console An electronic device with multiple inputs and outputs, used to combine, modify, and distribute the audio signal; the control point of the sound in a production; also known as **mixer, mixing board, pre-amp desk, sound board,** or **lighting desk.**

consular invoice A document certified by a consular official which describes a shipment of goods and provides information on the consignor, consignee, and value of the shipment and used by customs officials to verify the value, quantity, and nature of the shipment.

consular security manager See **Regional Security Officer (RSO).**

consultant An individual who provides business, professional, or expert advice for a fee.

consumer affairs An organization that controls and protects business name, trading hours, and practices.

consumer/trade show An exhibition open to the public usually requiring an entrance fee; also known as **gate show,** or **public show.**

consumer-quality equipment Video equipment designed for use by nonprofessionals, appropriate when the quality of the final product is not critical; used often for social events.

continental breakfast A morning meal consisting of pastries, juices, hot beverages, and fruit.

continental buffet A buffet consisting of pastries, juices, hot beverages, and fruit.

continental plan (CP)

continental plan (CP) A room rate that includes a **continental breakfast;** also see **bed & breakfast (B&B).**

contingencies Promises made in agreements or contracts that can be affected by future uncertainties; also allocated funds reserved in budgets for uncertainties.

continuing education credits (CEUs) Requirements of many professional groups by which members must certify participation in formal educational programs designed to maintain their level of ability beyond their original certification date.

continuity Smooth flow of action and narration from scene to scene.

Contract A legal agreement between two or more persons that creates an obligation to perform some act and establishes a mutual binding promise with penalty for failure to perform; also known as **commitment** or **letter of agreement.**

contractor A person who contracts to supply certain services or materials for a stipulated fee.

contractual liability Liability of another party assumed under contract or agreement as opposed to liability directly, as in tort.

contrast An opposition of intensity between light and dark areas of a scene.

contributed paper A written manuscript provided after acceptance of the **abstract** which becomes the basis for a speech or presentation; also known as **paper contribution.**

control track A section of video tape which controls the speed of the tape.

convener A person charged with welcoming and gathering participants.

convention A general and formal meeting of a legislative body, social or economic group to provide information on a particular situation and to establish consent on policies among the participants. Usually of limited duration with set objectives, but no determined frequency.

cordless/wireless microphone

Convention and Visitors Bureau A not-for-profit umbrella organization that represents a city or geographic area in the solicitation and servicing of travelers to that city or area whether they visit for business, pleasure, or both.

Convention Bureau A service organization which provides destination promotion and may offer personnel, housing control, and other services for meetings, conventions, and other events.

convention center A facility for events and expositions without sleeping rooms.

Convention Liaison Council (CLC) An organization whose members represent many convention industry organizations. The **CLC** conducts research, administers the **Certified Meeting Professional** (**CMP**) program, and discusses issues of common interest.

convention services manager/banquet services manager An employee of a facility or hotel who is responsible for the facility-related details of an event.

COO See **Chief Operating Officer.**

coordinating committee A committee created by the hosting organization(s) to plan, oversee, and ensure the creation of a successful event.

co-president One, two, or more people appointed to serve jointly as president on an equal footing with the official president.

copy Original text material being prepared for reproduction.

copyfitting/typesetting The process of determining space required and type size for copy to fit allotted space.

cordial An aromatic, syrupy liqueur often served after dinner; in Australia, a fruit-flavored, non-alcoholic syrup.

cordless/wireless microphone A portable microphone that operates on its own power source, connected to a radio transmitter; also known as a **vega** or **wireless microphone** or **radio microphone.**

corkage

corkage A charge placed on beer, wine, and liquor that is brought into a facility but purchased elsewhere and may include glassware, ice, and mixers.

corner booth An exhibit space with **aisles** on two sides; larger trade shows may add an additional charge because of the advantageous position.

corporate event An event sponsored by a corporation for the purpose of achieving specific goals and objectives such as entertaining customers, introducing and promoting new products or services, or providing incentives or training for employees, as well as other activities.

corporate meeting An officially sanctioned and required gathering of employees with travel, room, and meal expenses paid by the organization.

corporate picnics A business-sponsored picnic used to motivate employees through the fostering of goodwill. For associations, goals are to entertain existing members and solicit new memberships.

corporate planner An event manager employed by an organization to manage its events.

corporate rate A special room rate, lower than rack rate, for corporations that have made prior arrangements with the facility. Usually based on a certain commitment of rooms to be used in a period of time. Also known as **Commercial Rate.**

corporate theater The use of actors to dramatize a company's image, a new product, or the history of an organization.

corporate travel A market segment of business travelers paid at company expense.

cost charge per square meter/foot A basic charge for a particular unit of measurement.

couchette (KOO-shet) A sleeping berth in a day/night compartment on a European train.

cross-fade

Council for the Advancement and Support of Education (CASE) An organization whose members work in higher education or supply products and services for the higher education field.

count 1. Total number of attendees for a given period. 2. Total number of exhibitors for a given period.

courier 1. A European term for a travel professional who supervises arrival details and escorts tours. 2. A person who delivers goods.

cover 1. A table setting for one person. 2. A term often used for the number of waiters per person.

cover footage A series of generic filmed or videotaped scenes shot during a particular event shown primarily during general script dialogue.

cover shot A single, wide-angle shot giving a broad view of the location and action of a filmed or televised event; a safety shot; photo taken for front of magazine, newspaper, or book.

covers The actual number of meals served at a food function.

cover stock A heavy-weight paper used for protective and decorative purposes in binding a document.

crawl A text that moves horizontally across the bottom of a video screen.

credentials See **press pass.**

credits The names of the individuals who created or performed in an event, recording, film, or video.

crew Stagehands, technicians, truck loaders, and others responsible for the technical setup of a show.

crop A cutting technique which reduces the area of a photograph or art work.

cross-bar A rod used in draping or as a support brace.

cross-fade A smooth change from one color or image to another.

cross-fading A technique used to change scenes or images by fading out as another fades in; see **dissolve unit.**

crosstalk An undesired sound emanating from another channel or track.

crumbdown The process of a waiter removing table crumbs before the next course is served.

CSEP See **Certified Special Events Professional.**

cue A visual or audio signal to elicit response or action.

cue card An off-camera card containing text used by performers to read lines; also known as **idiot card.**

cueing The process of assigning cue numbers to various elements of a production.

Current New York Time (CNYT) A standard of time used in broadcast television to coordinate time differences for booking broadcasting facilities.

customs 1. Established social conventions of a country or region. 2. A government agency that controls entry of people and products into that country and charged with the collection of duties.

customs broker A person or company that provides customs-clearing services to shippers of goods to and from another country; see **Brussels Tariff Nomenclature.**

custom duties A fee paid for importing, exporting, or consuming of goods to a government agency; see **Brussels Tariff Nomenclature.**

cut 1. An instantaneous change from one scene to another without a fade or **dissolve.** 2. A visual or auditory signal to interrupt or cancel.

cut and lay The installation of carpet other than normal booth or aisle size.

cutline The text identifying a photograph.

cyc or cyclorama

cut-off date The designated day that a facility will release to the general public a block of guest/sleeping rooms that had previously been reserved.

cut-off time The hour at which a non-guaranteed reservation must be filled or may be canceled.

cyc or cyclorama A stage background scene that gives the illusion of depth.

daily newsletter Daily information sheet for participants during an event.

dais (DAY- is) A raised platform for seating prominent people at the head table; also known as **lectern, podium, rostrum.**

damask Woven silk or linen fabric used for tablecloths and napkins.

dance floor 1. An area for dancing that can be carpeted when not in use. 2. A portable surface for dancing that can be rented and assembled for events.

DAT cassette See **digital audio tape.**

data base A collection of historical information to be used for current or future planning.

date draft A bank document which matures a specified number of days after the date it is issued without regard to the date of acceptance.

dead areas A space in the event facility where sound is muffled or absent.

debate A discussion of opposing arguments or positions.

decorating The planning and furnishing of an exhibition or function with carpet, drapes, plants, stage sets, props, florals, etc., to create a pleasant, attractive environment.

decorator A general contractor or service contractor, usually hired to set up an exhibition and/or design and implement "the look" of an event. Also known as a **designer.**

definite booking Space reservations confirmed in writing.

delegate A voting representative at a meeting.

delegate card An admission card confirming a booking and registration.

Delphi An on-line service from General Videotext, the same people who run BIX, although the services are separate.

demi-pension

demi-pension A rate that includes a room, breakfast, and dinner; in the U.S. and Canada: **Modified American Plan (MAP)** which includes room, breakfast, and one other meal (usually dinner); also known as **halfboard**.

denied boarding compensation A refund of airfare or a payment to passenger when airline fails to honor a confirmed reservation within two hours of scheduled departure.

departure date The date when majority of event participants check out of a facility.

departure tax A fee collected from traveler by host country at time of departure.

deposit A partial payment to secure product or service.

deputy stage manager The assistant to the production stage manager.

design An artist's conception or rendering of how a printed piece or event should look.

designer See **decorator**.

dessert tray See **pastry cart**.

destination A city, area, or country which can be marketed to groups or individuals as a place to visit or hold a meeting.

destination management company (DMC) A company, based in the city, county, or state in which the event is being held, which handles service contracts, tours, ground transportation, decorations, props, and theme events; similar to **Professional Congress Organizer (PCO)**.

destination manager A local on-site coordinator.

detail drawing A drawing showing method of construction or specific element.

devaluation The official lowering of the value of a currency.

deviation The departure of an individual traveler from the established group itinerary.

dialogue A discussion of ideas and opinions between two or more persons.

die-cutting A process of cutting shapes into a sheet of printed paper stock. Used for cuts of paper not following a straight line.

diffraction grating A series of fine grooves that break down light into its component frequencies, as a prism does; it may also produce step-and-repeat patterns of scanned images.

digital audio tape (DAT) A product that uses digital instead of analog audio signals. Similar to a video tape.

digital recording 1. The process of sampling analog video or audio programs using an analog-to-digital (D/A) processor to produce a stream of binary-coded electronic signals numerically representing the content of the programs which are then stored on an appropriate device for retrieval at some later time. Once the video and audio programming material has been converted to a digital media format, the programs can be easily transmitted to other locations or copied to other media without further degradation to the quality of the recorded image or sound. 2. Refers to a video or audio program that was previously processed through an analog-to-digital processor and then stored for later playback using any one of a variety of media that employ binary recording techniques. Examples of commonly used, digital recording media that can be used to store video and audio programs are: compact digital audio disks (CD); compact digital read only memory disks (CD-ROM); **Digital Audio Tapes (DAT)**; and digital video disks (DVD).

dimmer An electronic device used to control light intensity.

dine around A restaurant term that indicates the use of a number of restaurants in a destination with reservations and billing arrangements for one particular client.

dinner The evening meal for an individual or a group, not usually ceremonial; also known as **supper**.

direct billing

direct billing Account receivables mailed to individuals or firms with established credit.

direct flight A flight between two points on the same aircraft; may be stops but no plane changes.

director of sales (DOS) The person in charge of operation and sale of sleeping rooms for a hotel; also known as **sales manager.**

directory See **function board.**

disco effects A variety of techniques used to light the dance floor with movable beams and changing color; less expensive than **intelligent lighting.**

discussion form An application to put a question to a particular speaker on a specific subject and submitted in advance of the conference session.

discussion group A group of participants in separate debates; similar to a working group but with no expectation of reports or papers.

discussion leader The person who introduces topics of discussion and mediates group discussion; also known as **moderator.**

dismantle To disassemble and remove exhibits, sets, or props.

dismantling deadline A designated day and time by which exhibits, sets, or props must be dismantled and removed from an exhibition area.

dispatcher A person responsible for scheduling and routing freight, labor, etc.

display builder A company which fabricates displays.

display case A showcase used to display and protect exhibit articles.

display fibers See **fiber optics.**

display material Articles exhibited for participants at meetings and conventions which may be insured or have value stated in writing for insurance purposes.

display place An exhibit booth.

display type 1. In printing, a type larger than **body type**. 2. A type of fireworks used for exhibitions and displays.

dissolve In a slide or multimedia presentation, to change from one scene to another by blending visual images together as one image fades out as another **fades in.**

dissolve unit A device which creates fade-out and **fade-in** of slides between two projectors; see **cross-fading.**

distributed sound Low to mid-level sound produced by locating a large number of speakers around a central listening area and used for background music, **soundscaping,** or to keep the sound level from being too loud.

district sales manager The person responsible for hotel room sales in a designated territory.

divergence The angle at which a laser beam widens, which has design implications for the user. For long throws, beam width at the final target may be critical. Low divergence is a plus but can be traded off sometimes to increase other assets, such as getting higher power from the same laser.

divider 1. Walls or light movable panels used for partitioning floor areas or concealing others; also known as **movable wall, partition, screen.** 2. Material that partitions a large meeting or function area into smaller ones; also known as **airwalls.**

diving walls See **Air Wall.**

DMC See **Destination Management Company** and **Ground Operator.**

DNS See **Domain Name System.**

docent A tour guide in a museum or art gallery.

dolly Low, flat platform on wheels used for carrying heavy loads.

domain name system (DNS) A multi-part naming system devised to avoid the crisis of naming hosts (individual computers) on the Internet. Host names are a string of words separated by dots.

domestic beer/wine A beer or wine produced in the country where it is served.

domestic meetings 1. Domestic/National: A meeting of an organization with membership from a single nation available to meet in only that nation. 2. Domestic/subregional: A meeting of an organization with membership from a single nation available to meet in only a given subregion of that nation.

donahue A style of presentation wherein the **moderator** moves among audience members with a **microphone** seeking questions and comments for a group of panelists.

donation A sum of money or items of value received as gifts for charity.

DOS See **director of sales.**

double bed A bed measuring 53" × 75".

double booking The practice of reserving space for two or more groups for the same dates when only one group can be accommodated.

double cloth The use of two tablecloths on a banquet table for decorative purposes.

double-double room A room with two double beds, suitable for two to four persons.

double lock The use of two locks on a door for extra security, one of which is often a dead bolt.

double room A room occupied by two persons that may have a *king, queen, double bed,* or two *single beds.*

double room for single occupancy A twin or double room occupied by one person, often charged at a lower rate than if occupied by

dry snack/nibbles

two people; in Australia room rate is normally based on room type, not the number of guests.

doubling   The playing of more than one instrument by a musician during an engagement.

downgrade   To move to a lesser accommodation or class of service.

downline space   The remaining flights on an itinerary.

down-linking   The reception of a satellite-transmitted signal.

downstage   The front of the stage, closest to the audience.

draper   A person who installs drapes, pleats, and special decor.

drapes/theatrical curtains   A decorative material hung to partition an area, adorn a room, or provide privacy.

draping   A fabric hanging used to create exhibit booths, to finish or surround an area such as an audiovisual screen, or provide a backdrop for a stage or wall; also known as **pipe and drape.**

drayage   The transfer of exhibit booths, equipment, materials, and properties from decorator storage to exhibit site.

dress   1. Clothing worn by talent. 2. Dress rehearsal; final camera rehearsal. 3. Set dressing; necessary set properties. 4. To neatly arrange cables lying on the floor.

drop   1. A large, painted piece of cloth used for stage background or scenery. 2. A term used to describe height of curtain.

dropout   Momentary loss of recorded audio or video signal during playback, due to imperfections in the tape.

dry lease   The rental of a plane without crew, supplies, fuel, and maintenance service.

dry run   The rehearsal or trial run-through of a program.

dry snack/nibbles   Snacks such as pretzels, potato or corn chips, popcorn, or nuts.

~ 55 ~

dual capacity The legal principle that a business may stand in relation to its employees not only as employer but also as supplier of a product, provider of a service, owner of premises, etc.

dual setup An arrangement of duplicate meeting-room setups in two different locations.

dub 1. To transfer recorded sound, video, or film from one unit to another. 2. A copy of a recording, video, film, or photo.

dummy 1. A paper mock-up of proposed printed piece. 2. A mannequin.

duo Two performers or musicians.

duotone A photograph prepared for two-color reproduction.

dupe (duplicate) A film or tape which is printed from the original copy.

duplex outlet A double electrical outlet.

duty manager See **manager on duty.**

duvetyne (DOO-va-teen) A soft, flexible fabric with a thick nap used for table covering and skirting.

Electret

early arrival 1. Guest arrival before confirmed reservation date and/or time. 2. Arrival prior to the majority of the group.

early-bird rate A special room rate for early registration.

easel A tripod stand with a rack used to hold magnetic board, posters, signs, charts, flip charts.

Easylink An electronic mail service formerly operated by Western Union and now operated by AT&T.

eaves 1. The perimeter of a tent roof where the side walls are attached with a wall rope. 2. The top edge of a *valance* curtain.

eaves troughing Canvas used to channel rain water away from a tent roof to the outside edge, like gutters on a building.

ECU European Currency Unit.

EDAC See **Exhibit & Display Association of Canada.**

editing To prepare or revise final copy before publication.

EDPA See **Exhibit Designers & Producers of Canada.**

educational Events comprised of people employed or working within the educational industry.

educational program The total educational selection offered during an event.

educational visit Educational tour of a work place, manufacturing plant, or other facility of interest to a conference; also known as **study mission.**

effects device An electronic device placed in an audio system and used by the mixer to create special effects and control sound level and quality; also known as a **limiter, reverb, or equalizer.**

efficiency 1. A guest room with kitchen facilities. 2. Self-contained or self-serviced apartment.

Electret See **condenser microphone.**

electric cart An electric-powered vehicle used by crew and staff at large events and in convention halls; also known as **scooter.**

electric pointer/ laser pointer An electric device used by a speaker to cast an illuminated spot of light to draw attention to a particular feature being demonstrated.

electrical contractor A company contracted by event management to provide electrical services.

electronic editing A process by which program elements are inserted and assembled on audio tape without physically cutting the tape.

electronic pour An electric system of dispensing an exact amount of liquor per drink.

elevated table A counter-height table used in a registration area to provide a writing surface.

elevation The front and side views of a drawing.

ellipsoidal spotlight (I-LIP'-soid-l) A lighting instrument containing shutters and allowing for the use of a **gobo** to project patterns or text.

elite A type size that produces twelve typed characters per inch.

embossing 1. Impressing letters or artwork in relief to produce a three-dimensional effect. Blind embossing is an inkless impression on blank paper.

endorsement To give approval or agreement to a certain subject matter or event.

energy break A refreshment break where nutritious foods and beverages are served, occasionally including exercise.

engineering A department responsible for keeping a building in physical working condition, including repair and maintenance of the electrical system, lighting, temperature control, and general repair.

errors and omissions insurance

English breakfast/full breakfast A morning meal consisting of hot cereal, eggs, meat, pastries, preserves, juices, hot beverages, and fruit.

end sections The roof sections forming the ends of a sectional tent; for example, a sectional 60' × 120' tent has two end sections that, when put together, form a 60' × 60' tent. Adding three 20' center sections results in the full 120 length.

English service A style of banquet service where an elaborately prepared main course is first displayed on a rolling cart before it is served.

entertainment An activity performed for the enjoyment of others.

entertainment provider A specialist who assesses entertainment needs and provides talent booking services for events.

entrance canopy An awning from a permanent building or from a main tent to the driveway or street that enhances the visual effect and provides shelter for guests.

entree 1. A dish served as the main course of a meal. 2. In Europe and Australia, the appetizer.

EPO See **pay own.**

epergne (E-purn) A vertical pedestal, with attached vases or bowls, to hold floral arrangements and serves as a centerpiece for a table.

equalizer An **effects device** used to compensate for undesirable sound system characteristics or room acoustics. See **effects device.**

erase The electronic removal of program elements from a recorded tape.

erection Assembling exhibits and displays or tents on site.

errors and omissions insurance A liability coverage which protects the **event management** consultant from financial risk due to mistakes or oversights he or she may have made that cause physical, financial, or other injury to additional parties.

ESCA   See **Exposition Service Contractors Association.**

E-shaped setup   A configuration of tables in a meeting room arranged in the shape of an **E** with chairs placed on the outside of the closed end and on both sides of each table leg.

estimate   A preliminary calculation of the cost of work to be undertaken.

ETA   An abbreviation for estimated time of arrival.

ETD   An abbreviation for estimated time of departure.

Eurodollars   U.S. dollars placed on deposit in banks outside the U.S.

European Currency Unit (ECU)   The currency unit of the European Community.

European plan/room only (EP)   A room rate that does not include meals.

evaluation   1. Critiquing and rating the overall success of an event. 2. Developing an event profile gathered from accurate event statistics at the completion of the event.

event management   1. The function requiring public assembly for the purpose of celebration, education, marketing, and reunion. 2. The process that includes research, design, planning, coordination, and evaluation of events.

event manager   The individual responsible for researching, designing, planning, coordinating, marketing, and evaluating an event.

event marketing   The process that integrates a range of marketing elements around a central event sponsorship or lifestyle-themed activity. This process incorporates advertising, employee and consumer programs, sales promotion, public relations, causes, business to business, television property, and trade promotion with a specific event or events.

event order (EO)/running sheet/running order Detailed instructions for an event; also known as **function sheet, banquet event order,** or **résumé.**

example See **scenario.**

excess baggage Luggage which exceeds the allowance set by the airline and requires a fee.

exciter lamp Lamp which projects illumination through the optical sound track on 16mm film. Light patterns are read by the projector sound head, converted to electronic signals, and fed to an audio amplifier.

exclusion A provision of an insurance policy which stipulates specific prohibitions (hazards, circumstances, and property) to coverage.

exclusive contractor A contractor appointed by show or building management as the sole agent to provide services.

excursion 1. A journey made with the intention to return to the original point of departure. 2. A recreational trip provided as a scheduled portion of the event program; also known as **tour.**

executive committee A committee created to decide policy and strategy for the organization of an event; also known as **management committee.**

executive secretary A person appointed to handle organizational functions and given certain administrative authority and responsibilities.

exhibit booth A display area constructed for exhibitors to showcase their products or convey a message.

exhibit designer/producer An individual or company responsible for designing and constructing exhibit booth.

Exhibit Designers & Producers of Canada (EDPC) A Canadian organization whose members are designers and producers of exhibits of events in Canada.

exhibit directory

exhibit directory A program or catalog listing exhibitors and exhibit booth location.

Exhibit & Display Association of Canada (EDAC) An organization for exhibitors at conferences and events in Canada.

exhibit hall The area within a facility where exhibition is located.

exhibition A display for public view of products or promotional materials for the purpose of public relations, sales, and or marketing; also known as **exposition** or **industrial show,** or **trade show.**

exhibition area See **booth/stand area.**

exhibition contractor The organizer or promoter of an exhibition responsible for the letting of space, financial control, and management.

exhibition manager An individual responsible for coordinating exposition.

exhibition plan A plan showing space occupied by exhibitors, including the areas for booths/stands, passageways, and services.

exhibition prospectus A pamphlet for potential exhibitors and other interested parties on the conditions, technical points, cost of exhibition space, floor plan, and application for participation.

exhibit manager 1. The person in charge of an individual exhibit booth. 2. The show management staff member in charge of an entire exhibit area.

exhibitor A company or organization sponsoring an exhibit booth.

exhibitor's kit A kit prepared and sent by exhibition organizer to all registered participants containing information and supplier request forms or names of local contractors; also known as **service kit, exhibitor's manual.**

exhibitor's manual See **service kit** or **exhibitor's kit.**

exhibit prospectus Promotional materials and published specifications, rules, and regulations provided for prospective exhibitors and designed to encourage participation.

extra section

exploder An electrical apparatus used to ignite fireworks.

export license A government document which permits the "licensee" to engage in the export of designated goods to specified destinations.

exposition 1. An event at which products and services are displayed for public view. Also known as **exhibition.** 2. An assembly of a large number of individuals to discuss items of mutual interest or engage in professional development through learning activities.

exposition service contractor A supplier of booth equipment, including rental furnishings and floor coverings, labor, **drayage,** and signs for **expositions** and **trade shows.**

Exposition Service Contractors Association (ESCA) An organization whose membership provides services and products within the exposition industry,

exposure The state of being subject to loss because of some hazard or contingency.

extended type A type that is wider than standard type and allowing fewer characters per line.

extinction The removal of unwanted portions of a laser graphic by **blanking.**

extraordinary session A special session for activities, needs, or situations that are different from those normally and originally scheduled.

extra section An aircraft or bus added to accommodate a group's planned transportation needs.

FAA See **Federal Aviation Administration.**

fabrication The construction of an exhibit or display.

FAC See **Federal Airports Corporation.**

facilitator A trained mediator who guides discussion and decision making in small group meetings.

fade-in To change gradually from a dark screen to a visual image; also known as **dissolve.**

fader A device used to control all dimming circuits.

fair A public celebration that includes commercial and civic activities.

false bow A staged bow and exit by the artist with a planned return pending audience response.

FAM See **familiarization trip.**

familiarization trip (FAM) A program designed to acquaint participants with specific destinations or services and to stimulate the booking of an event offered to potential buyers of an event site; also known as **inspection trip.**

family name The preferred form for international registration documents in place of "last name"; see **given name.**

family plan A discount price offered by hotels and resorts to families consisting of two or more members traveling together.

family style service A style of serving in which guests serve themselves from platters and bowls of food placed on the table.

fan A laser effect in which a pencil-thin laser beam is moved rapidly from side to side creating the appearance of a sheet of light. By mixing up-and-down motion with the side-to-side motion, laserists can create a variety of fan effects.

FAP full American plan; also known as **American Plan.**

fascia 1. A panel displayed at top of exhibit indicating company name. 2. A hard skirting applied to a stage.

fascia board Hard panel used to display information or screen a stage or event area.

fashion show A choreographed display of garments by models.

FC See **Financial Controller**; also known as **chief financial officer**.

Federal Airports Corporation (FAC) An organization responsible for creating and enforcing the rules and regulations for airplane landings.

Federal Aviation Administration (FAA) A U.S. federal agency responsible for creating and enforcing the rules and regulations for flying.

fee A charge for registration and permits; a sum paid for admission; a payment for a professional service.

feedback A regeneration of sound from audio speakers back through a microphone causing a squealing sound.

feeder space Reservations for passengers from home city to **gateway city** for international flights or flights to Hawaii; see **stub space**.

festival A public celebration that conveys through a kaleidoscope of activities, certain meanings to participants and spectators.

fete An outdoor **festival**.

fete stall A two by four meter tent used as a booth.

fiber optics/fibre optics Very thin, transparent glass or plastic fibers encased in a material with a lower index of refraction that transmit light through internal reflections. Transmission fibers move laser light from its source to a remote location without showing a light path. **Display fibers** glow, like neon wire, when laser light is passed through them.

Fidonet (FI-do-net) A large, electronic worldwide **bulletin board system (BBS)**.

field production The shooting of rough footage early in film production; at this point the **storyboard** is established during preproduction and followed to ensure all bases are carefully covered.

File Transfer Protocol (FTP) A program on the **Internet** that allows users to transfer files between computers. Many **Internet** nodes (individual computers) contain files that are available to the general public through anonymous **FTP**.

fill light Light used to fill shadows created by **key light**.

film chain A series of projectors and video equipment transmitting projected materials through a television system.

film clip A brief piece of film shown from a larger film production to elicit interest.

film report A conclusive summary of conference events.

filmstrip A series of slides reproduced on one continuous strip of film.

filter 1. A coated glass used to separate or combine colors within the optical section of a laser projector, by transmission or reflection. 2. A paper cartridge used to strain particles of dirt from laser-cooling water. 3. Special equipment used in still and motion picture photography and video to create specific optical effects. 4. A color filter or gel used in front of light.

final program/blueprint A document containing the definitive conference program, distributed to participants prior to or at the commencement of an event.

financial controller (FC) See **chief financial officer**.

financial procedures An outline of accounting and banking techniques.

financial report Document incorporating the statement of income and expenditure and the budget at a given date.

financial responsibility law A statutory provision requiring owners of automobiles to provide evidence of their ability to pay damages arising out of automobile operation.

Finger A service on the **Internet** that can provide information about the person associated with a particular user identification.

finger bowl A dish of hot water, sometimes scented and accompanied by fresh linen, presented after or during a meal or course, to cleanse the hands and lips.

fire exit A means of egress regulated by a local regulations to ensure safe exit during an emergency.

first aid 1. Emergency care or treatment given before a doctor arrives. 2. The location where emergency health care is provided by licensed medical personnel.

first announcement An initial notification of an event outlining the basic framework of a meeting which is a widely circulated to potential participants; see **preliminary announcement.**

first option See **option.**

fishpole A long pole with a microphone often used in question-and-answer sessions.

fixed seating arrangement Chairs in meeting rooms which are permanently mounted to the floor.

fixed theater The permanent, non-movable seats in a meeting room or amphitheater.

flag carrier 1. An airline carrier designated by a country to serve international routes. 2. An individual carrying a flag or banner in a procession.

flame-proof A material used to retard flammability in clothing and construction materials.

flash A technique of blinking a slide on and off to add emphasis.

flash box A smoke-producing device for special effects.

flash pot A pyrotechnic device which simulates a **flash.**

flat rate One price based on average cost, for all guest/sleeping rooms in a hotel exclusive of suites; may be flat-rate single or flat-rate double; also known as **run-of-the-house-rate.**

flip chart A large pad of paper placed on an easel and used by a speaker for illustrative purposes.

floater/casual A temporary worker(s) used to assist permanent workers for short periods of time.

floor load/loading The maximum amount of weight per square foot a floor can support.

floor manager 1. A person retained by management to supervise the exhibit area. 2. A television technician who directs and cues the talent during studio operations.

floor marking A method of marking booth space.

floor plan 1. A schematic drawing of a room including its dimensions and design, used to develop event plans.

floor set-up diagram A detailed floor plan drawn to scale showing the specific setup requirements for a meeting or function, including the dais, tables, and chairs.

flop To reverse a photo or illustration so that it conforms to the basic design.

floppy disk A diskette on which a computer file or program is created or stored.

floral designer A professional who specializes in designing with floral materials and decor.

flush A style of typesetting even with right, left, and/or both margins; see **justified margin.**

fly The objects and scenery hanging from above.

flyer A one-piece printed announcement or advertisement of a special event, distributed as a handbill or by mail.

foam core Two sheets of lightweight specially coated paper sealed on either side of a styrofoam center, used for signs, decorating, and exhibits.

focal length 1. The distance from the center of a lens to the film plane. 2. The size of a lens required to obtain a specific size picture.

focus 1. Proper sharpness of the outline of an image. 2. Pointing of lights to a specific area.

foil-stamping Metallic or colored "foil leaf" used in stamping printed matter. Heat and pressure are used to print the design on a surface.

folio A form on which all charge transactions incurred by a registered guest are recorded.

follow spotlight A spotlight mounted to a yoke that can swivel, allowing an operator to pan and tilt the beam to follow the movement of a performer; generally contains an adjustable iris, shutter, and a color changer for further alteration of the beam.

font An assortment of type of one style and size.

food and beverage director A person in a hotel who manages all activities related to food and beverage.

force majeure clause (force MAY-shure) Contract clause which limits liability should the event be prevented due to disruptive circumstances beyond the sponsor's control, including war, strikes, catastrophic weather; see **Act of God**.

forecast 1. To predict a hotel's occupancy situation on any given date. 2. The projected revenue of a facility for a given period of time.

foreign independent tour (FIT)/free or fully independent traveler A custom-designed prepaid tour for an individual traveler.

foreign meeting A meeting comprised of attendees from other nations; also known as **international meeting** or **institute**.

foreign/national Membership of meeting participation available to organizations or individuals from one nation, but able to meet in another nation.

forklift A vehicle with a power-operated pronged platform for lifting and carrying loads; see **tow motor**.

formal dining service See **butler service (Australia)**.

formal dress See **black tie**.

forum An open discussion between audience, panel members, and moderator.

forward contract A financial instrument guaranteeing a specific rate of exchange in a foreign currency for a future transaction.

four color separation A photographic process utilizing four colored screened patterns from which printing plates can be engraved.

four hour call A minimum work period for which union labor must be paid if called to work.

foyer Public or pre-function area in hotel or hall for assembly or registration.

frame An individual picture in a filmstrip, motion picture, or video.

frame tent Professionally installed tent consisting of a canvas or vinyl top stretched over a metal frame and containing no center poles.

fraternal A group associated by common personal interests rather than common job or career responsibilities.

free form Self-supporting and independent exhibit material.

free paper A presentation of a written transcript given after acceptance of the abstract on a subject chosen by the author.

free papers session Reports on topics that strictly relate to the meeting theme, but are closely related and are held in a separate session.

free pour The preparation of alcoholic drinks by hand without the use of a shot glass or other measuring utensils.

free trade zone A port area designated by a government for duty-free entry of non-prohibited goods, which may be stored, displayed, or used for manufacturing within the zone and exported without paying duty. Duties are imposed on the goods and manufactured items only when the goods pass from the *zone* into an area subject to **customs**.

freeze frame A motion picture or video frame that is stopped so that the single frame is displayed; see **stop motion**.

freight See **cartage**.

freight forwarder 1. A business that handles export shipments for compensation. 2. A company transporting goods from one site to another (interstate, international).

French action A curtain which opens from the center.

French (silver) service A style of banquet food service serving each food item from a platter to an individual plate.

fresnel A lighting instrument that uses a **fresnel** lens to produce a diffused, soft-edged beam. The spacing between the lamp and the lens can be adjusted to alter the beam spread from spot to flood.

front desk 1. An area in a hotel where guests check in and out, room assignments are made, and the final guest bill is paid. 2. The center of meeting facility activities, including registration and cashier services.

front screen projection The projection of an image onto the front surface of a light reflecting screen from a projector placed within or behind the audience.

FTP See **File Transfer Protocol**.

full American plan (FAP) See **American plan**.

Full Board An inclusive fee for room, all meals, and tax and service charges. See **inclusive rate**.

full booth coverage A carpet covering the entire area of a booth.

Full Breakfast Full morning meal. See **American breakfast.**

full coverage Any form of insurance that provides payment in full of all losses caused by the perils insured against to the limits of the policy.

full house A term which indicates that guest rooms are occupied or committed; see **closed/fully booked.**

function bill (account) An itemized invoice prepared by the hotel stating the charges for each function of an event.

function board An area where announcements are listed with the day's events; see **directory** or **reader board.**

function book A journal used to record the assignment of event space within a venue.

function sheet A document that records the details of an event's needs; including sleeping rooms, billing arrangements, food, beverages, and audio-visual equipment, and is distributed to all hotel departments and the event organizer; also known as **resume, banquet event order,** or **event order.**

function space A facility area where private functions, meetings, or events can be held.

fund raising The activity or profession of obtaining money for charitable organizations.

fund raising event An event whose purpose is to raise funds for a charitable cause and to identify new sources of support.

funnel flight An air trip requiring a change of planes at an intermediate stop while maintaining the same flight number.

future bookings An event or meeting that is reserved during a specific time period and scheduled for a future date in a specific location.

General Agreement on Tariffs and Trade (GATT)

gaffer's tape A vinyl, impregnated fabric tape used to anchor cables to the floor among other purposes.

gain The level or degree of audio volume; see **level.**

gala dinner The outstanding social event of a conference including a formal meal, speeches, and entertainment.

galley proof Typeset copy for an author's review and correction before printing.

galvo See **scanner or galvanometer (laser).**

Gangway 1. See **aisle.** 2. A connecting **bridgeway** between two points.

gap analysis An analytical tool used to identify gaps in the design of an event. For example, an outdoor event planned during the rainy season would produce a gap that could be closed with either a tent or an indoor location.

garment rack A metal frame that holds apparel.

garni To adorn or decorate food.

garni, hotel A hotel without dining facilities.

garnish A food decoration, usually edible, which adds color and form to food presentation.

gate show See **consumer trade show** or **public show.**

gateway city A city with an international airport.

GATT See **General Agreement on Tariffs and Trade.**

gel A colored transparent material placed in front of a lighting instrument to color the light.

General Agreement on Tariffs and Trade (GATT) A multilateral treaty whose purpose is to help reduce trade barriers between the signatory countries and to promote trade through tariff concessions.

general contractor

general contractor Company which can provide all services to exhibition management and exhibitors.

general export license Any of various export licenses used to export commodities requiring formal application or written authorization.

general session A meeting open to all; also known as event participants; **plenary session.**

GEnie An on-line service run by General Electric, GEnie is the consumer portion of GE's commercial on-line service dating back to the 1960's.

geographic segmentation The arbitrary division of a market by country, region, state, zone, district, standard metropolitan statistical area (SMSA), or city.

gerb/fountain A pyrotechnic device that displays a 2" to 2' flame depending on its diameter; see **lance.**

GIT See **group inclusive tour.**

giveaway (or novelties) 1. An advertising specialty item, imprinted with a logo or an event theme, freely given as a keepsake; see **amenity.** 2. A gift or item for sale imprinted with an event's logo and theme.

given name The preferred form for "first name" for international registration documents; see **family name.**

glass beaded screen A type of screen surface used for **front-screen projection;** see **beaded screen.**

goblet A drinking glass with stem and foot.

gobo A metal or glass template inserted into a focusable lighting fixture used to define projected light patterns; it does for a lighting designer what a stencil does for a sign maker.

gofer (GO-pher) A person hired to act as a runner/messenger.

goodie bag A container for gifts given to guests at the end of an event.

gridlock

good one side/surface quality   A piece of plywood or decorative material whose face side is free of blemishes.

Gopher   A distributed service on the **Internet** that can organize and provide access to hierarchically related information. The information can be in various forms: library, catalogs, databases, news groups, etc.

go to black   An entertainment term meaning to turn off the room light or change the light gradually from an image to a black screen.

government events   A public function to acknowledge significant community change, including ground breakings, inaugurations, and dedications of public buildings.

government meetings   A gathering of groups of civil servants, elected officials, or service providers to governmental entities.

grand opening   A celebration marking a new place of business or first day of operations of a public venue to which potential customers and important contacts are invited.

grandstand   See **bleachers.**

graphics   1. Illustrations, photographs, layouts, combined with type style and copy. 2. Simple line images, which can be abstract patterns, drawings, or words.

gratuity   A tip for service; see **perquisite** or **bonus.**

green room   A room, stocked with refreshments, for an artist, honored guest, or speaker and entourage to relax or meet guests and media representatives.

Greenwich Mean Time   The mean solar time determined at the prime meridian at Greenwich, England, used as the standard basis of time throughout the world; see **Zulu Time.**

gridlock   See **shoehorn.**

grip

grip 1. A stagehand who assists a master carpenter. 2. A general assistant in the film industry.

gross square feet A measurement of area determined by multiplying the width by the length.

gross weight The full weight of a shipment, including goods and packaging.

ground breaking The ceremonial turning of the first piece of earth at a construction site to promote the project and the product or service to be produced.

ground operator A company or person in *destination* city handling local transportation and other local travel needs; see **DMC**.

groundrow Freestanding, low scenery, or a painted cutout which provides an illusion of depth and masks unsightly views.

group booking A reservation for a block of rooms specifically for one group.

group inclusive tour (GIT) A travel program with special fares and specific requirements; i.e., minimum number of persons traveling as a group throughout the tour.

group rate A negotiated guest/sleeping room rate for a group.

GTD See **guaranteed number.**

guarantee The number of food and beverage servings to be paid for regardless of whether actually consumed; usually the number of servings must be relayed by the host to the caterer forty-eight hours in advance of the event.

guaranteed late arrival/guaranteed arrival A guest room secured by credit card or advance payment to ensure reservation is not canceled for the evening.

guaranteed number (GTD) Servings, meals, or rooms requested and paid for whether actually consumed or occupied.

guaranteed reservation A prepaid reservation held until agreed arrival time or check-out time the next day, whichever occurs first, making the guest responsible for payment if reservation is not canceled.

guest list A list of peoples' names invited to and/or attending a function and usually indicating table seatings.

guest/sleeping room A sleeping room for event attendee or participant.

guide A person accompanying a tour who provides detailed knowledge of places of interest.

guy ropes Ropes that extend from the eaves of a tent to each side pole and then to anchors in the ground, providing support for the roof.

half board See **demi-pension** or **modified American plan (MAP)**.

half moon table Two quarter-round tables attached to make a half circle.

half-round step A 60" to 72" round table with seating only around the half of the table facing the speaker or stage.

half-time spectacle Events designed to entertain spectators midway through a **sports event**.

halftone A photograph that has been prepared for single color reproduction.

hall A large room for public assembly.

hallmark A major one-time or recurring event of limited duration; see **mega event**.

handout Information provided during sessions which pertains to the subject being discussed.

hand truck A small hand-propelled implement with two wheels and two handles used for transporting small loads.

hard disk A disk within a computer that serves as its permanent memory.

hardwall booth A stand or booth constructed with plywood or similar material, as opposed to a booth formed by drapery only.

hardware Computer equipment.

head 1. A pan-tilt device on which a camera is mounted. 2. The part of the laser that includes the tube and emits the beam; the other part of the laser is its power supply, connected to the **head** by an umbilical cord. 3. The XY scan output of a laser; a laser projector may support one or more of these heads. 4. The video or audio device which records or reads the electronic signals from the video or audio tape.

head count The total number of people attending an event.

headquarters hotel A facility which serves as the center of operations where registration, general sessions, and the conference staff office are located.

headset Headphones with a built-in microphone.

head table 1. The most visible area to seat **VIPs** and the **master of ceremonies** at a function. 2. The seating location for honored guests and/or presenters at events.

head tax A fee charged to arriving and departing passengers in some foreign countries.

HCEA See **Health Care Exhibitors Association.**

Health Care Exhibitors Association (HCEA) An organization whose members exhibit health care products and services or provide products and services to health care exhibitors.

helium-neon (HeNe) A mixture of two gasses inside a laser tube which creates a warm red color.

herringbone setup A configuration of tables and chairs angled in a V-shape facing the head table, stage, or speaker; see **V-shape setup** or **chevron.**

hertz (Hz) Unit of frequency equal to one cycle per second.

hidden charge Unbudgeted expense.

highball glasses A tall glass used to serve an alcoholic mixed drink.

high jacker A piece of equipment capable of elevating one or several people to a given height; see **cherry picker** or **scissor lift.**

high-key lighting A lighting technique in which picture intensity creates limited dark areas.

high season The periods or seasons when traffic or volume is highest; see **peak season.**

high-tech visuals Visual presentations involving sophisticated, equipment like lasers, or multi-image and mixed media equipment.

hospitality suite

hip The external angle formed by two sloping sides of a tent roof when quarter poles are used as supports.

historical report/guest history report A report that gives history of a group attending an event.

History The record of an organization's previous meetings; usually containing information pertaining to the room block, actual room pickup, meeting space required, and food and beverage revenues generated.

hold harmless A contract clause that ensures that a group or company will not be responsible in the event of a claim.

hold harmless agreement A contractual agreement whereby one party assumes the liability inherent in a situation, thereby relieving the other party of responsibility.

holiday events Celebrations marking annual civic, religious, or legal holidays such as Christmas or Independence Day.

hollow circular setup A circular configuration of tables with chairs placed at the perimeter and the center remaining empty.

hollow square setup A configuration of tables in a square or rectangle with chairs at the perimeter and the center remaining empty.

home page The starting page when a user "visits" a **World Wide Web** local site on the **Internet.**

honorarium A payment made to recognize an individual who has played a key role without the expectation of a fixed fee.

honorary An appointment made without the expectation of full participation or payment of dues, often in recognition of expertise or past work.

horseshoe setup A configuration of tables in a *U-shape*, with chairs placed outside and sometimes inside; see **open-U Setup** or **U-shape setup.**

hospitality suite A room or suite used to entertain guests.

host 1. An organization, association, corporate body, city, country, or other such party that initiates an event to take place within or under its jurisdiction and at its financial responsibility. 2. An individual or organization that issues an invitation for persons to attend an event. 3. Each individual computer on the **Internet.**

host bar A private bar at which drinks are paid for by a **sponsor;** the opposite is a cash bar; see **open bar.**

hotel accommodation form A hotel booking form provided for event participants; showing arrival and departure dates and type of room and rate; see **reservation form.**

hotel classifications The ranking of a hotel in terms of its amenities, facilities, level of service, and cost, which include deluxe, luxury, first class, superior, standard, economy, and budget. Qualifications and terms may vary by country.

Hotel Sales and Marketing Association International (HSMAI) An organization providing information and resources to its members who are international sales marketing persons of hospitality firms and agencies, and those who provide products and services for hospitality sales and marketing professionals.

hot microphone/camera A microphone or camera that is open and working.

hot spot An undesirable concentration of light on one area of slide or film.

hot tag VIP Luggage tagged for special handling.

house account An expense account used for miscellaneous incidental expenses that are not chargeable to an event or another hotel account.

house board A switch panel which controls all electrical fixtures.

house brand A medium- or lower-priced brand of liquor used when a particular brand is not specified.

housekeeping A facility department which provides daily maid and cleaning service in addition to irons, ironing boards, hair dryers, laundry, and other items as requested by guests.

housekeeping announcements Announcements about schedule changes, locations of functions, and similar program information.

house lights Room lighting that operates separately from stage lighting.

house manager A person in charge of the auditorium or the entire facility but not the stage production.

house plan A diagram depicting the function space in a facility.

house wines The standard wines offered by a facility usually at lower cost.

housing The process of assigning hotel sleeping rooms to attendees.

housing bureau A reservation office within a convention bureau which coordinates housing for groups.

HSMAI See **Hotel Sales and Marketing Association International.**

hue A color or gradation of color.

human resources event A conference or session used to motivate, educate, or develop human resources within an organization.

hummingbirds In pyrotechnics, a short tube packed with an explosive which propels the device creating a strong jet flame in a straight pattern while emitting a buzzing sound.

hyper-cardioid (CAR-di-oid) microphone A unidirectional microphone with a tight, long-reaching pattern that accepts only a narrow angle of sound, enabling the pickup of distant voices for question-and-answer sessions, as well as for choirs; see **shotgun microphone.**

Hypertext A computer technology that can handle text, graphics, and sounds.

impaired vision seating

IAAM See **International Association of Auditorium Managers.**

IAB See **Internet Architecture Board.**

IACC See **International Association of Conference Centers.**

IACVB See **International Association of Convention & Visitors Bureaus.**

I & D To install and dismantle.

IAEM See **International Association for Exposition Management.**

IANA See **Internet Assigned Numbers Authority.**

IATA See **International Association of Travel Agents.**

IATSE See **International Association of Theatrical Stage Employees.**

IBEW See **International Brotherhood of Electrical Workers.**

ICCA See **International Congress and Convention Association.**

ice carving A decorative piece or logo carved from ice.

ICPA See **Insurance Conference Planners Association.**

ID sign A placard which identifies a booth's exhibitor.

idiot cards Hand-written placards which display script to performers; see **cue cards.**

IEA See **International Exhibitors Association.**

IFEA See **International Festival and Events Association.**

IHO An abbreviation for "in honor of".

ILDA See **International Laser Display Association.**

illumination Lighting available in hall, built into exhibit, or available on a rental basis.

impaired vision seating See **obstructed view.**

import license A document required and issued by governments authorizing the importation of goods.

inauguration ceremony An official ceremony marking the induction of officers that often includes an address by a dignitary or a symbolic gesture.

incentive A reward offered to stimulate greater effort.

incentive event A corporate-sponsored meeting or trip to reward performance, motivate work effort, and create company loyalty; often built around a theme.

incentive meeting/trip A corporate-sponsored event which is offered to reward outstanding performance.

incentive travel A corporate-paid trip offered as a prize to stimulate productivity.

incentive travel company An agency that designs, sells, and coordinates **incentive travel** programs.

incidental entertainment See **sight acts.**

incidentals All expenses other than room charge and tax billed to a guest's account, such as room service and telephone calls.

inclusive Catering or accommodation rates that include gratuities and taxes.

inclusive cost A quoted cost often for food and beverage functions to which no extra costs are to be added.

inclusive rate 1. The amount charged for a room, meals, taxes, and service charge; see **American plan (FAP), full board,** or **modified American plan (MAP).** 2. Charges for food and beverages, including taxes, gratuities, and/or service charges.

inclusive tour A group trip that includes costs, such as admission fees, transfers, and most gratuities.

indemnification Insurance protection from a loss under stated circumstances or a reimbursement for liabilities.

institute

industrial show An exhibit of related or similar products by various companies for the purposes of introducing new products, sales promotion, and increased visibility to the general public; see **exhibition, exposition,** or **trade show.**

informal dress See **business attire.**

infringement 1. The use of floor space outside the exclusive **booth area.** 2. Use of copyright without permission.

inherent flame proof Material that is permanently flame resistant without chemical treatment for theatrical and stage use.

in-house A term referring to corporate, event, and travel services located within and staffed by the company.

in-house services Those services (audiovisual, florist) available within an event facility.

in-plant A term referring to corporate travel services located within but staffed by an outside travel agency.

inquiry cards Requests collected from exhibit attendees or readers of trade magazines for further information about products and services.

insert 1. A matted or framed portion of a picture. 2. Additional shot added to a scene at a later time. 3. Additional promotional material included in mailing or publication.

inside booth An exhibit space surrounded by other booths or stands at both sides and the back.

inside booth stand An exhibit space with **booths/stands** at back on each side.

inspection trip See **familiarization trip.**

installation The activity of setting up exhibit booths and related services according to instructions and drawings.

institute In-depth instructional meeting comprised of attendees from two or more countries and located outside the national borders of attending countries or within the borders of one of the participant nations; see **foreign meeting** or **international meeting.**

insurance A contractual relationship that exists when one party, for a consideration, agrees to reimburse another party for loss to property, life, or person caused by specified contingencies, i.e., fire, accident, death.

Insurance Conference Planners Association (ICPA) An organization providing information, education, and resources to professional conference planners in the insurance industry and those who supply products and services to *insurance conference planners.*

in sync The concurrence of two or more audio and/or visual events.

intelligent lighting A remote-controlled theatrical lighting instrument whose beam can spot or go to flood, vary from bright to dim, move horizontally (**pan**) and vertically (tilt), and change color. All of these operations can be computer programmed to allow for very rapid and precise changes. A series of **gobo** patterns also are built into the fixture.

interactive response A system which enables the audience to respond at their seats to prepared questions by means of a multi-function keypad. Responses are fed to a computer which tabulates them and displays the results graphically on a **projection screen.**

intercom An audio system permitting two-way local communication with a microphone and a loudspeaker at each end.

intercontinental meeting See **international meetings.**

interline connection An airline connection which involves transferring from one airline to another and baggage is automatically transferred; see **off-line connection.**

interlock The synchronization of two or more sound and/or picture sources.

International Association of Auditorium Managers (IAAM) An organization providing information and resources for its members who represent auditorium managers, arena stadium managers, and other event facilities and those who provide services and products for this industry.

International Association of Conference Centers (IACC) A trade association whose members are conference centers worldwide.

International Association of Convention & Visitors Bureaus (IACVB) A trade association providing resources, education, and information to members who represent **convention and visitors bureaus** worldwide and those who provide products and services for conference centers.

International Association for Exposition Management (IAEM) A trade association that provides information, education, and resources to members representing exposition management and managers worldwide, and those who provide services and products for this industry.

International Association of Theatrical Stage Employees (IATSE) (eye-ah-tzee) A trade union representing professional theatrical stage hands all over the world.

International Association of Travel Agents (IATA) (eye-AH-ta) A trade association providing information and resources to travel agents all over the world who deal with international trade and those who provide products and services for this industry.

International Brotherhood of Electrical Workers (IBEW) A professional union of electrical workers.

International Congress and Convention Association (ICCA) An organization providing information and resources to members involved in the coordinating of congresses and various categories (such as hotels, congress centers, airlines, and professional congress organizers) within the travel and hospitality industry.

International Exhibitors Association (IEA) An organization providing information, education, and resources to members who are exhibitors and those who provide products and services for the industry.

International Festival and Events Association (IFEA)

International Festival and Events Association (IFEA) An organization providing information, education, and resources to members who are festival and event managers and those who provide products and services for this industry.

International Laser Display Association (ILDA) An organization providing information, education, and resources to members who are involved in laser design and production and those who provide products and services to this industry.

International Meeting 1. International/Intercontinental: A meeting of an organization with multi-national membership that is available to meet on more than one continent. 2. International/Continental: A meeting of an organization with multi-national membership that is available to meet on only one continent. 3. International/Regional: A meeting of an organization with multi-national membership that is available to meet in only a given region of one continent. 4. See **foreign meeting** or **institute.**

International Special Events Society (ISES) (eye-sis) An organization providing education, certification, resources, and information to its members who are professional event managers and those who provide services and products to this industry.

Internet An electronic network connecting millions of computers with information technology. An **Internet** work, which is a computer network consisting of two or more smaller networks that can communicate with each other.

Internet address The name or the number of a **host** machine that identifies it on the **Internet**. The mailbox is usually one's user name and location.

Internet Architecture Board (IAB) Formerly the *Internet Activities Board*, this organization oversees, with the help of the **Internet Assigned Numbers Authority,** standards and development for the **Internet** and administrates the **Internet** subtree in the global tree in which all networking knowledge is stored.

ISES

Internet Assigned Numbers Authority (IANA) An **Internet** organization responsible for assigning values for networks, attributes, etc. Operated by the University of Southern California Information Sciences Institute, it verifies that the same identifier values are not assigned to two different entities.

Internet Relay Chat (IRC) A service on the **Internet** that extends **talk** capabilities to allow multi-party conversations.

Internet Society (ISOC) An international organization that promotes the use of the **Internet** for communication and collaboration.

interpretation in relay An oral translation utilizing two interpreters because the first is not master of the language, and requires that another makes the final interpretation to the audience.

interpreter's booth/stand A soundproof cabin in which an interpreter works.

inventory The total amount of furniture and equipment available for a show.

invitation program A provisional program sometimes incorporating a **call for papers** and may include information on location, participants, agenda, and accommodations.

invited speakers 1. A person invited to deliver a speech whose fee, travel, and housing expenses are paid. 2. A prospective speaker who has not been confirmed.

invocation A prayer given at the beginning of an event function. The benediction is given at the end.

involuntary upgrade An airline term used when a passenger is moved to a higher class at no charge.

IRC See **Internet Relay Chat.**

iris A circular lens diaphragm found in cameras which regulates the entry of light onto film. Variable aperture (opening of lens).

ISES (eye-sis) See **International Special Events Society.**

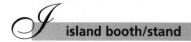
island booth/stand

island booth/stand Four or more exhibit spaces with aisles on all four sides.

ISOC See **Internet Society.**

itinerary A detailed schedule of a visit or tour.

justified type

jacket A clear plastic covering used to protect slides or badges.

janitorial service Service offered to exhibitors for cleaning **booths/stands** and for general cleaning for event sites.

jigger A standard measure of liquor of 30 mls, approximately one and one-half ounces.

jigger spouts An adapter for a liquor bottle that delivers a pre-measured amount, usually one and one-half ounces.

job tender See **bid manual specifications.**

Johnny Carson setup/host interview setup An arrangement for a panel discussion with the moderator's desk perpendicular to the panelists' chairs.

joint fares Through-fare for travel on two or more airlines.

Jughead A service on the **Internet** that helps make certain **Gopher** searches easier and more manageable.

justified margin See **flush.**

justified type A style of type set with both margins adjusted with type and spacing to be equal; see **flush.**

krypton

keg A bulk container for beer or wine, which affords better pricing.

Kelvin (K) 1. A scale used to measure absolute temperature with zero equal to −459.4° Fahrenheit. 2. A scale on which the unit of measure equals the centigrade degree and according to which absolute zero is 0°, the equivalent of −213.16° centigrade.

key light The principal source of illumination on a subject or area.

keynote speaker A speaker who sets forth the theme or tone for the event.

keystoning A distortion of a projected image.

king room A room with a **king-size bed** suitable for one or two persons.

king-size bed Large bed usually measuring 76" × 80" (190 × 200 cm); long king-size bed measures 76" × 84".

kiosk 1. A small enclosure for ticket sales, information, etc. 2. A freestanding pavilion or lightweight structure with one or more open sides.

kit See **service kit**.

klieg light A slang term taken from the brand name for a variety of outdated spotlights.

knockdown (KD) An unassembled exhibit requiring on-site assembly.

krypton The gas placed inside a laser tube that creates a cool red color or a mixture of red, green, blue, and yellow.

labor call   A method of securing union employees through the local union.

labor desk   An on-site area from which service personnel are dispatched at an event such as an exposition.

labor form   A form used by exhibitors requesting labor at an exhibition.

lace line   The joint or seam between roof sections where one is joined to another. **Tents** are generally made up of several roof sections fastened together with heavy zippers or jackknife-type lacing through grommets.

lamp   A light source for a projector or lighting instrument.

lamp life   The estimated hours of a lamp's life.

lanai (la-NI)   A hotel or resort room with a patio or balcony overlooking a garden or water.

lance   In pyrotechnics, a short paper tube packed with an explosive that displays a two-inch flame of color for 30 to 45 seconds.

landscape (horizontal)   A sign whose width is larger than its height.

lapel microphone   See **lavaliere microphone.**

laser   A device that produces an intense ray of deeply colored, bright light, about ⅛" thick as it emerges from the laser. The tube is filled with a noble gas, which determines its emitted color(s) which it does when excited electrically. The construction of the laser tube causes the light to become parallel, pure, and intense.

late registration   A *booking* received after a stated deadline, and usually imposing a penalty fee.

lavaliere microphone (la-VA-leer)   A portable monodirectional microphone that hooks around the speaker's neck or is attached with a clip; usually not visible to the audience, it frees the speaker's hands and allows for movement; see **lapel, necklace,** or **pendant microphone.**

layout An artist's or designer's depiction of how a printed piece will look.

leader A utility tape added to an audiotape or film to create a visual starting point.

lead time The time prior to a meeting or other key event during which work is to be completed.

le cafe table See **cabaret table.**

lectern A stand upon which a speaker may rest notes or books. A piece of furniture that rests on the floor, a standing **lectern,** or a "table top" that is one-half the size of a standing lectern and rests on a table.

lectern microphone An amplifying device that is attached to a lectern; see **cardioid microphone.**

lecture An informative or instructional speech.

legal connection A minimum time regulated by the **Federal Aviation Administration** to leave one flight and board another.

Leko (LEE-ko) A slang term derived from *Lekolite,* a lighting instrument manufactured by Century Lighting, commonly used for any ellipsoidal reflector spotlight. A **Leko** contains a movable lens that enables the beam to be focused with either a hard or soft edge; a group of internal shutters allows the beam to be cropped, and many **Lekos** have an adjustable iris that allows a variation of the beam diameter. **Lekos** can accommodate a pattern holder containing a **gobo** for projection of a specific image.

lenticular A type of screen surface used for **front projection,** characterized by tiny corrugations or grooves molded or embossed into the screen surface.

lessee The person or organization to whom a lease is given.

lessor A person or organization that offers a lease.

Letrasign A trade name for self-adhesive vinyl letters used to create signs.

letter of agreement   A document outlining proposed services, space, or products which becomes binding upon written approval by both parties; see **contract** or **commitment.**

letter of credit (L/C)   A document issued by a bank per instructions from a buyer of goods, authorizing the seller to draw a specified sum of money under specified terms.

level   See **gain.**

liability   A legal responsibility to make good a loss or claim.

lift truck   See **forklift.**

lightface   A typeface distinguished by light, thin lines.

lighting   A service offered by a production or lighting company for lights or special effects for stage, theater, or venue.

lighting control console   Desk-type housing used to contain the controls required for adjusting production lighting; also known as **master control.**

lighting desk   See **console.**

lighting director   A person who designs the lighting, directs placement of lighting equipment, and calls lighting cues on-site.

lighting grid   A structure used to support lights and electrical outlets.

light organ   An electronic device that allows sound waves to determine the color or intensity of lighting.

light table/Kelvin box/light   An illuminated glass-covered table used for viewing and editing slides, transparencies, and art/layout graphics.

limiter   See **effects device.**

limits of liability   The maximum amount an insurance company agrees to pay in the case of loss and, therefore, the most an insured may collect by the terms of the policy.

linen A collective term for tablecloths and napkins; also known as **napery**.

line of sight An unobstructed line of vision from audience to stage; also known as **sight line**.

liqueurs A spirit or wine-based liquor highly sweetened and flavored with an aromatic substance; also known as **cordials**.

list of exhibitors A list of exhibiting firms usually indicating location which may be arranged alphabetically, by category, or both, and listing personnel in attendance.

list of participants A register of delegates and accompanying persons attending an event.

liter (or litre) A metric unit of measure equal to approximately one quart.

live operation The operation of a laser device by a trained operator from a real-time control device.

load factor 1. The maximum weight allowed by a venue for hanging equipment from ceiling or supporting floor equipment. 2. An average number of airline or other transportation seats occupied.

loading dock The area on premises where goods are received.

load in/out The scheduled time for a crew to load and unload equipment.

lobby A public area that serves as an entrance or waiting area.

local beer/wine Beer or wine produced and served locally.

local event A function that draws its audience primarily from the local market.

local host A group of people who carry out the strategies and policies established for the organization of an event; see **organizing committee**.

luncheon

lockout 1. Refusal by a facility to allow guests access to their rooms. 2. Refusal by owners to allow employees to return to their jobs following a strike.

lock-up 1. A storage area which can be secured. 2. A jail or temporary holding area at venue for suspected criminal.

logo 1. A symbol identifying an organization or event. 2. A trademark used exclusively by one company or association.

lost business A business or contract not secured.

lower case Small letters, as distinguished from capital letters.

low-key lighting Lighting in which picture intensity produces limited bright areas.

low season The time of year when travel and hotel rates are at their lowest.

lumina A nebulous effect produced by transmitting laser light through a textured plastic.

luncheon A noonday meal, sometimes accompanied by speeches or presentations.

magnetic sound A sound that is recorded on magnetic tape and may be incorporated into a film.

mail and messages A place where mail and messages are kept or transmitted; also known as **message center.**

main tent A room or hall where business sessions and entertainment productions are held.

maitre d' (MAY-tra-dee) The floor manager or head waiter at a restaurant or catered function; also known as **banquet captain** or **supervisor.**

management committee See **executive committee.**

manager on duty (MOD) The person at a hotel or conference center who is currently in charge; also known as **duty manager.**

MAP See **modified American plan.**

march A demonstration wherein an organization or group walks a specified route/distance to promote a cause and bring attention to specific issues.

marker board A white surface on which washable color markers are used.

market The potential consumer group likely to be interested in or need a service or product.

marketing The activity of research, planning, and coordinating strategies to sell products or services.

marketing flights A series of advertising or public relations events all relating to the same marketing effort or theme.

market segments A categorization of an organization or business by professional discipline or primary area of interest for the purpose of sales analysis or assignment.

marks See **spike marks.**

marquee (mar-KEY) A long and narrow tent without sides used for sheltering walkways or defining an entry to a tent or to seat guests. In Australia, Great Britain, and other countries this term means **tent.**

mask 1. A scenic drape used to obscure undesirable views from the audience. 2. To partially cover the output aperture of a laser projector to circumscribe the laser field to conform to a screen area and to trap the laser output if it strays from its intended path, protecting the audience from accidental exposure to direct laser scanning.

masking drapes The drapes used to cover storage, backstage, and other unsightly areas.

master The original, best quality, and final edited version of an audio tape, a video tape or film recording of a production; also known as **master tape.**

master account An organization's account to which approved facility expenses can be charged during a designated stay.

master control See **lighting control console.**

master key A key that will open all function rooms, guest rooms, and facility areas.

master monitor A video monitor which shows only the picture being presented for broadcast.

master of ceremonies See **MC.**

master tape See **master.**

matte white A type of screen surface used for front projection, characterized by a rough surface free from shine or highlights.

MC (em-CEE) An individual who introduces persons or elements of an event; see **compere, master of ceremonies, moderator,** and **toastmaster.**

MCI Mail A large, commercial e-mail system on the **Internet.**

medical meeting A meeting focused on health care, medical research industries, or medical professions.

mega event See **hallmark.**

meeting An assembly of individuals gathered to discuss items of mutual interest or engage in professional development through learning activities.

Meeting Professionals International (MPI) An organization providing education, representation, information, and resources to its members who plan meetings or provide services and products to meeting planners.

meet the press setup A **panel** setup with questioners placed opposite guest panelists and moderator.

message board A board on which messages are displayed and often includes communication among attendees of an event.

message center See **mail and messages.**

microphone 1. A basic element of all sound systems; it causes sound waves to be generated or modulated using electrical current and transmits or records sound; also known as a **mike.** 2. Instrument which converts sound into electrical signals and is the primary input for all sound systems.

middle of the road (MOR) A mixture of contemporary, top 40, and soft music.

mike See **microphone.**

military meeting A meeting attended by members of the armed forces or suppliers to the armed forces.

minimum The smallest allowable number of **covers** and/or beverages for a function: a surcharge may apply if **minimum** is not reached.

minutes A formal written record of a meeting.

mirror ball A large sphere with small mirrors fixed over its surface which revolves when electrified. When a spotlight is lit and

 mirrors

focused upon the ball, it creates a mass of small light beams that swirl around the room.

mirrors   Reflecting material used for laser lighting; *scanner mirrors* are tiny, lightweight, and heat resistant and used to reflect and guide laser light to create a graphic. *Beam-sculpture mirrors* are larger and mounted at a distance from the laser projector so that beams can be bounced off them to create beam sculptures.

misconnect   A term used to indicate that insufficient time is allowed for connection between planes, as regulated by the FAA.

mix   1. Visual: a repetitive and/or alternating projection of two different slides on the screen used to add emphasis. 2. Sound: an adjustment of each input for volume and sound quality.

mixer   1. An audio engineer, the technician who operates the **console** controlling the audio mix and level of a production. 2. In **audio-visual** recording, devices by which sound from all microphones feeds into one system and required if three or more microphones are used in one room. 3. **Splits** that go with alcoholic beverages. 4. Also known as a **console** or **pre-amp desk.**

mixing   The technique of combining audio and video sources.

mixing board   See **sound board.**

MOD   See **manager on duty.**

moderator   A person who presides over sessions, panels, and forums; also known as **compere, discussion leader, MC,** and **Toastmaster.**

modified American plan (MAP)   A room rate which includes two meals, usually breakfast and **dinner** although lunch is sometimes substituted for **dinner;** also known as **demi-pension** or **half board.**

modular exhibit   An exhibit constructed with interchangeable components.

modular panels   Partition units (walls, door frames, etc.) in standard sizes used for building **booths/stands** in the sizes desired.

monitor 1. A television set with direct audio and video input. 2. A **speaker** used by performers to hear music on stage.

monitor mixing console A **sound board** used to regulate and mix sound heard on stage.

monochrome A single color image such as those reproduced on a black and white television.

montage 1. A composite image made by combining several separate pictures. 2. A rapid succession of images to illustrate an association of ideas.

MOR See **middle of the road.**

movable wall See **airwall.**

move-in The date and time set for installation of exhibits, decorations, and other equipment by exhibitors and decorators; also known as **bump-in.**

move-out The date and time set for dismantling of exhibits and other equipment by exhibitors and decorators; also known as **bump-out.**

MPI See **Meeting Professionals International.**

multi-channel A term indicating two or more communication bands (receivers).

multi-image A visual presentation technique using more than one projected image at a time; also known as **multi-screen** or **multi-vision.**

multimedia The use of two or more audiovisual media in one presentation; usually audio material is synchronized with visual image presentation.

multi-national meeting An international meeting with a minimum of 100 participants from at least four countries.

multiplexer A unit designed for selective projection of 16 mm film, 2" × 2" slides, or filmstrips, into one television program.

multi-screen See **multi-image**.

multi-vision See **multi-image**.

Murphy bed A retractable bed built into the wall.

music stands Sheet music holders of varying sizes requiring attached lights when used on darkened stage.

mylar The trade name for a shiny, plastic material used for balloons and decorations.

NACE See **National Association of Catering Executives.**

name tag An identification label worn by a delegate indicating name, company, and title.

napery See **linen.**

napkin folds Napkins folded decoratively.

National Association of Catering Executives (NACE) An organization of professional on- and off-premise caterers and their suppliers that provides education, resources, and information.

National Coalition of Black Meeting Planners (NCBMP) An organization providing education, resources, and representation to its membership of black meeting planners and others who provide services and products for their meetings.

national dress See **black tie** and **formal dress.**

national meeting A meeting of organizations or individuals from one nation and meeting in that nation; also known as **domestic meetings.**

National Tourist Office (NTO) An official government agency that promotes country tours and activities and provides information services to visitors.

NCBMP See **National Coalition of Black Meeting Planners.**

near-plant A term which indicates a company's travel reservations may occur at a travel agency or at the company and actual ticketing occurs at the travel agency branch; also known as Converted Inplant.

neck (or necklace) microphone See **lavaliere microphone.**

negative A reversed image of art or type.

negligence The failure to use that degree of care which is considered reasonable precaution under given circumstances.

netnet or nett/nett The actual cost of an event excluding mark-ups or commissions.

net or nett square feet The actual amount of salable space available for exhibit booths.

Niagara Falls In pyrotechnics, a set of **gerbs** chained together with fuse and rope, set and hung so that a white color is displayed downward, creating an effect of a waterfall at night.

nodes Individual computers on the **Internet** that make up a network; also known as **stations.**

non-commissionable A type of sale in which a percentage of the sale amount is not paid to the agent or purchaser.

no-op An airline flight not operating.

non-sked An airline offering charter service on a non-scheduled basis.

no-show Hotel, airline, or meeting reservations made, but not kept without notice or canceled according to guidelines.

non-stop flight A flight from one city to another with no stops.

NTO See **National Tourist Office.**

number stands Stands used to hold numbers designating specific event activity areas.

OAG   See **Official Airline Guide.**

obstructed view   A blocked view of the stage as seen from audience seating; also known as **impaired vision seating.**

occupancy rate   The percentage of total number of available sleeping rooms actually occupied, derived by dividing the total number of rooms occupied during a given time period (night, week, year) by the total number of rooms available for occupancy during that same period.

occurrence   An accident, including continuous or repeated exposures to substantially the same general harmful conditions.

off-camera   A performance or action not seen on camera, such as a narration.

Official Airline Guide (OAG)   A geographically categorized publication providing information on airline schedules, airports, connecting times, etc.

official carrier   An airline company designated as the preferred transport for an event in exchange for special rates or services.

official contractor   A general contractor chosen as the main vendor for an event.

off-line connection   See **interline connection.**

off-line editing   The editing of a film or videotape that involves cuts and splices only and no special effects. An economical process that provides time to plan and organize **on-line editing** and helps avoid wasting valuable time and effort.

off-premise caterer   A professional caterer who specializes in providing food and beverage services to locations outside a normal facility, i.e., tents, museums, office buildings, sound stages, open fields, parking garages, empty warehouses, or event facilities that allow outside catering.

off-season   A term which indicates the facility occupancy is at its lowest level.

off-shore meeting

off-shore meeting A meeting occurring in a country outside the originating body.

off-site event An activity scheduled away from a facility.

offset 1. A photographic printing process. 2. The unwanted transfer of freshly printed wet image onto back of another sheet of paper.

offstage A term indicating a stage area which is not in view of the audience.

oil cloth A material used for signs and banners.

oil cracker A compressor that forces air into a chamber containing pure oil breaking down molecules and creating a very fine mist that enhances lighting beams.

omnidirectional microphone A microphone that picks up sound from all directions, used in **lavalieres** and for conferences; not recommended for entertainers.

one for fifty or 1/50 A complimentary room policy which offers one complimentary room night for every fifty room nights picked up; normally not to exceed four or five rooms.

100% star billing A contractual requirement by an artist that his/her name appear in a type style and size equal to or greater than other names in advertising and promotional materials.

one shot An exhibit or display fabricated for one-time use only.

on-line editing The editing of film or videotape done at a facility equipped to handle special effects and maximum manipulation of the material. The most expensive form of editing, it ultimately offers greater visual opportunities.

on-premise caterer A caterer who provides food and beverage service to a specific facility, such as a convention hall, hotel, or banquet facility.

on-site order Floor order placed at venue.

on-site registration The process of signing up for an event on the day of or at the location of the event.

original language

open   Rooms which are available for sale or occupancy.

open bar   A private room bar setup where drinks are paid for by a sponsor; usually including a full range of spirits; also known as **host bar,** or **sponsored bar.**

open end   An unlimited number of winners eligible for **incentive travel.**

open house   An event held at a place of business to provide customers, peers, members, the public, the media, or employees' families a first-hand look at a facility, products, and the way business is conducted.

opening ceremony   The formal opening session of an event; also known as an **opening session.**

opening session   See **opening ceremony.**

open ticket   A ticket valid for transportation between certain points, indicating no specific reservation date or time.

open-U setup   See **horseshoe setup** or **U-shape setup.**

optical sound   A sound that is recorded by photographic means on film.

option(s)   1. Space, products, or services reserved but not yet contracted for, with the right of refusal to confirm a tentative space reservation if there is demand from another group; also known as **first option,** or **tentative hold.** 2. Activities other than those included in the formal agenda which are not required and often demand the payment of an additional participation fee.

order of preference   A system which ranks dignitaries according to international protocol for purposes of seating, honors, or ceremonies.

organizing committee   See **local host.**

original language   The initial language in which a document is drafted or a speech is delivered.

OT

OT See **overtime.**

outlets Restaurants and lounges within an event facility.

out of order An event room or facility space or equipment under renovation or requiring maintenance.

outside exhibit A booth located outdoors.

outside line A telephone line from in-house to the outside obtained through the in-house operator.

outtake Taped or filmed scenes deleted from the final production.

overage A surplus, excess, or extra.

overbook The activity of accepting reservations for more guest rooms, aircraft seats, or services than are available in anticipation of **no-shows;** see **oversold.**

overflow Hotel **guest/sleeping rooms** booked by planner for attendees at other locations after headquarters facilities are full.

overhead projector A piece of audio-visual equipment which produces a magnified image on a vertical screen by passing light through a horizontal transparent slide or other transparency.

overlay 1. A decorative cloth used to dress a banquet table. 2. A clear acetate film used to separate different components of artwork. 3. A tissue sheet over artwork on which corrections or alterations are indicated.

overset A number of places set for a food event in addition to the guaranteed amount.

oversold The number of confirmed reservations which exceed the number of seats on an aircraft; see **overbook.**

overtime Labor-work performed in excess of 40 hours per week; also known as **OT,** or **rostered times.**

overview See **scenario.**

package A conference or tour arrangement combined and sold at a single all-inclusive price.

package plan A management practice of providing furniture and/or services to exhibitors for a single fee.

paid-out The amount of a cash withdrawal requested by the event organizer and charged to the facility's **master account,** often used to set up registration cash boxes.

pallet A wooden platform used for storing and transporting equipment; see **skid.**

pan Sideways movement of a camera to film or videotape wide scene.

panel A format for discussion by a moderator and two or more panelists.

panorama The widest view of a scene.

paper contribution See **contributed paper.**

parabolic aluminized reflector lights (PAR lights) Unlike **fresnels** and **Lekos,** the reflector and the lens are built into the lamp of the **PAR light,** rather than being part of the instrument's body. Lighting instrument available in beam spreads from a very narrow spot to a wide flood.

parabolic projection screen A type of front projection screen surface that when stretched is very rigid and allows only narrow angle viewing.

parade A moving pageant including floats, bands, individual entertainers, and dignitaries.

PAR Lights See **parabolic aluminized reflector lights.**

parlor A room usually equipped with couches that make into beds and connected to a suite bedroom.

participant A person performing an assigned role in a program or event; frequently used incorrectly to mean attendee; also known as a **program participant.**

partition See **airwall**.

party canopy A lightweight covering supported by one or more centerpoles designed to shelter against the sun or light rain, usually supplied as an inexpensive do-it-yourself tent rental.

passport A government document issued to a citizen permitting travel to another country and the right to re-enter the country.

paste-up An arrangement of type and illustrations on an art board used as camera-ready art.

pastry cart A serving technique used to select a dessert by display on a rolling tray; also known as a **dessert tray**.

PA system See **public address system**.

patch 1. To temporarily join wires or slides by overlapping. 2. A plug-in connection between two lines.

patch panel A plug and jack assembly permitting studio outlets to be temporarily connected to dimmer output circuits.

patron A person with a greater level of giving who heads a list of supporters.

patronage The trade or business given to a particular business.

payment authorization An officially sanctioned signature which authorizes payment of an invoice.

payment order A written authorization for payment to be made; also known as **purchase order**.

pay own A term which designates that each guest pays own guest charges; also known as **POA** and **EPO**.

PBX/PABX Operator A telephone switchboard operator.

PCMA See **Professional Convention Management Association**.

PCO See **professional congress organizer**.

personal manager

peak night An event management term referring to the night during an event when the most guest/sleeping rooms are used by those in attendance.

peak season An event industry term which indicates the busiest season when facility occupancy is at its highest level; also known as **high season.**

pendant microphone See **lavaliere microphone.**

pending registration An incomplete registration meaning the fees, full payment, or forms have not been received; also known as **provisional registration.**

peninsula booth/stand A configuration of two or more exhibit spaces placed back to back with an aisle on three sides.

penthouse suite Guest rooms and suites which are the largest and best rooms and often located on the top floors of the facility.

per diem (per-DEE-um) A fixed amount of funds available each day to a traveler to cover meals and expenses.

perfect binding A binding process in which pages are glued together at the indicated margin.

performance bond A legal instrument guaranteeing payment if contractual specifications are not met.

perimeter booth/stand An exhibit space located on an outside wall; also known as **backwall booth** or **booth/stand.**

permanent exhibit space Showrooms, marts, or similar space leased on a long-term basis for product displays.

per person An allowance of food and/or beverages purchased for an expected attendance.

perquisite A payment, benefit, or privilege received in addition to regular income or salary; also known as a **bonus** or **gratuity.**

personal manager A person who represents an individual artist or group of artists.

PERT See **Program Evaluation and Review Techniques.**

PERT chart An organizational flowchart defining responsibilities, due dates, and other information.

phased budget See **budget, budget chart, cash flowchart.**

photo opp See **photo opportunity.**

photo opportunity A type of press release tailored to a visual medium using a brief description of the visual nature of the event; known as a **request for coverage** when delivered to electronic media; also known as **photo opp.**

photo stats See **stats.**

piano types The designation of piano size and quality; i.e., concert grand, baby grand, spinet, table grand, upright, or electronic keyboard.

pica (PIE-ca) A size of type that produces ten typed characters or spaces per inch.

pick-up The number of facility guest rooms actually used out of a room block.

pin beam A narrow beam of light up to 20', usually produced by a small, 25-watt lamp and used to light banquet-table centerpieces, mirror balls, and dance floors; also known as **pin spot.**

pin poles See **side poles.**

pin spot See **pin beam.**

pipe and drape A system of aluminum poles supported by heavy metal bases which support lightweight fabric or vinyl where masking is required as in trade shows or stage productions; also known as **draping.**

pit A sunken area in front of the stage used to accommodate a musical group.

pitch 1. The slope of the roof of a tent resulting from the difference in height between the center poles and the side poles. 2. The distance between rows of seats of an aircraft. 3. A type size/spacing.

place card A small card placed on the banquet table inscribed with the name of the person designated to sit at that place.

plants Fresh, potted plants used as floral decor to enhance appearance of event.

plateau A level, stage, or tier of an **incentive travel** program at which a sales goal has been reached and a participant can then advance to a higher tier by additionally qualifying or purchasing the difference.

plated buffet A selection of prepared foods and entries set on a buffet table, which are chosen by the guests and served by a waiter.

plate microphone A flat semi-directional condenser microphone, sensitive to input when placed on a floor, wall, or Plexiglas panel; used for musicals, plays, group choirs, or low-profile situations where the microphone should not appear obvious to the audience; also known as **boundary microphone** or **PZM**.

platform A raised horizontal surface, stage, or flooring.

play-on/off Music which accompanies a performer's or speaker's entrance/exit onto or from the stage.

plenary session A general assembly for all participants; also known as **general session.**

plus-plus (++) 1. The addition of taxes and gratuities to a price when not included, designated by ++. 2. The additional fees for expenses provided to entertainers or speakers. 3. See **rider**.

POA See **pay own.**

podium The platform on which a speaker stands; also known as **dais, riser, rostrum,** or stage.

Point A measurement of type size; i.e., 12 points equal one pica, or approximately ⅙".

point-of-purchase

point-of-purchase A product display where sales can be made.

point source See **single-source sound.**

pole drapes Curtains hung from the upper section of the **center poles** of a tent to hide them and any guy ropes, stakes, or anchors.

pole tent A heavy-duty tent made of canvas or vinyl supported by poles at the perimeter and center. Pole tents require installation by professionals and will shelter against most bad weather.

pop-up canopy A small, lightweight, collapsible frame canopy with a fabric covering which provides shelter and protection from light rain and usually provided as a do-it-yourself rental tent which may be erected and removed quickly.

port 1. A fortified wine developed in Portugal and usually served after dinner. 2. The telephone to be used during a teleconference (one phone equals one port).

port of call A destination where boats arrive and depart with people and merchandise.

port of entry A destination providing customs and immigration services.

portrait A sign with greater height than width.

positive The exact image of copy as distinguished from reverse image or negative.

post 1. A metal upright used to support drapes. 2. The process following shooting a film or video where editing takes place.

post-con See **post-event briefing.**

post-conference registration A registration for an activity or function which follows a event.

post-conference reservation A **guest sleeping** room space held following a conference.

power

post-conference tour An organized outing taking place after the working conference for both **participants, attendees,** and **accompanying persons.**

post-event briefing A meeting between the event manager, key hotel staff, and possibly suppliers after the main event to debrief and critique the planning process and actual implementation; also known as **post-con.**

post-game event An event designed to attract and entertain spectators and fans immediately following a **sport event.**

post-graduate course Continuing education provided for professional accreditation purposes and designed to enhance and reinforce professional knowledge; also known as **professional program.**

poster A visual presentation of a specified size, presented on a flat sheet of paper or card with details of a specific topic.

poster board Soft panel used for displaying copy and/or graphics.

poster exhibition An area dedicated to the display of posters depicting research findings.

poster presentations An informal session held near poster exhibition to present and discuss content of posters.

poster session 1. A visual display of reports and papers, usually scientific, accompanied by authors or researchers. 2. A segment of time dedicated to the discussion of the posters shown inside the event area. When this discussion is not held in a special session, it can take place directly between the person presenting the poster and interested delegate(s).

post-trip A tour, optional extension, or side trip package offered after an event, gathering, or convention.

power 1. The electricity needed to supply the event. 2. In laser technology, the brightness of the laser light which is measured in watts. A ten-watt laser is enormously powerful compared to a ten-watt light bulb because the light bulb radiates light in every direction, whereas the laser directs the same amount of light onto a tiny area.

power amplifier   An electrical device used after a **console** to drive speakers and establish volume and consumes the largest amount of electrical power in the sound system; also known as an **amp**.

power of attorney   A legal document which allows one person to act legally on behalf of another person.

practical demonstration   A special setting for the demonstration of specific methods.

pre-amp desk   See **console** or **mixer**.

pre-assigned seating   1. The event-planning technique of predetermining seat assignments. 2. The procedure for requesting and receiving specific airline seats at time of reservation.

pre-con   See **pre-convention briefing**.

pre-conference   An organized outing taking place before the working conference for both **delegates, attendees,** and **accompanying persons**.

pre-convention briefing   A meeting with planner, facility department heads, and key suppliers to review the purpose and details of the upcoming event; also known as **pre-con**.

pre-fab   A pre-built exhibit ready for installation.

pre-function space   An area adjacent to the main event location where receptions and registration often take place.

pre-game event   An event designed to attract and entertain spectators and fans prior to the official start of a **sport event**.

preliminary announcement   See **first announcement**.

preliminary program   A second mailing introducing conference inducing information on program structure and key speakers, giving details of the ancillary conference activities and normally containing the conference registration forms; also known as **provisional program.**

premium   Merchandise available for purchase at discount by advertiser in order to promote products.

premium beer   A higher priced beer.

premium brand   Brands of liquor listed by a hotel or an establishment which are the most expensive brands at that establishment.

pre-opening   A period of time before a business' **soft opening.**

prep area   A space designated for preparation of food or displays, not visible to event **participants,** guests, and/or clients.

prepaid ticket advice (PTA)   An airline form stating that payment has been made.

preparation of paper   See **author's guideline/kit.**

preparatory session   A meeting of a specific group before the official assembly in order to finalize preparations.

pre-pleated   Fabric which is permanently pleated and ready for installation.

Preproduction   The organizational phase of a film or video project, including preparation of the concept, script, **storyboard,** and budget and crew, properties, and location are hired and determined. Traditionally, this is the most important phase of the project.

pre-registration list   A document of names of people pre-registered for an event versus on-site registration; also known as **printout.**

presenter   A person discussing and explaining a given topic in an educational session.

pre-set   The arrangement of food, usually salad, cold entree, or dessert, on banquet tables prior to the seating of guests.

press attaché The title given to the person handling all press and media activities, excluding advertising; also known as **press officer.**

press clipping/cutting An article cut from a newspaper or magazine.

press conference Interview granted to the media to announce major information. Since all media will be receiving the same information simultaneously, there will not be a chance for exclusivity, so personalized coverage should be provided for editing, including several spokespeople, visual displays, adequate question-and-answer time, and time for individual interviews.

press day An invitation to the media to cover an event before it is open to the public to promote the upcoming event; also known as **press party,** or **press tour.**

press gallery An area set aside for photographers, both still and video, which provides an unobstructed view of an event, as well as an adequate power supply and protection from the elements.

press hot line A designated direct telephone line reserved exclusively for the media.

press kit 1. A collection of items providing pertinent data on the meeting i.e., agenda, historical data, guest speakers, special events, etc. and on the facility such as photos, descriptions of public areas, and local entertainment, etc. 2. A kit that includes information relative to a sponsor's products or services.

press office An agency that collects and distributes information to the news media.

press officer See **press attaché.**

press party See **press day.**

press pass An identification symbol that allows free, unrestricted entry to an event by media personnel and allows staff to provide them with attention and assistance; also known as **credentials.**

press release A prepared statement released to targeted news media which succinctly provides information for immediate release or for release at a specified time or date.

Professional

press room An area reserved for media representatives with telephones, office machines, or a separate space for radio and television interviews.

press tour See **press day.**

pre-trip A tour, optional extension, or side trip package conducted before a meeting, gathering, or convention.

print A copy of the final edited film.

printout A documentary copy generated by a computer; also known as **pre-registration list.**

priority rating system A method of assigning **booth** space.

proceedings An official published volume transcribing full conference sessions which may or may not include details of any discussion.

procession A group of individuals moving in an orderly, often ceremonial manner.

Prodigy A very large on-line system on the **Internet** run by IBM and Sears.

producer A person responsible for entire live or electronic stage production.

product launch An event used to introduce or market a new product.

production schedule A detailed outline of all activities and tasks required to produce an event, deadlines for each action, and assignments to the individual, department, or committee responsible for specific acts; also known as **timeline.**

production tape A direct copy of the **master tape** used for rehearsal and production so the **master** will not be damaged; also known as a **show tape.**

Professional 1. Of or having to do with a profession. 2. Relating to organizations whose membership hold common professional credentials or interests. 3. Undertaken by professionals rather than amateurs. 4. A person who makes a business or trade of something that others do for pleasure.

professional congress organizer (PCO)   The European term for an event manager.

Professional Convention Management Association (PCMA)   An organization providing education, information, and resources to members who are meeting planners or those who provide service and products for meetings.

professional program   See **post-graduate course.**

program   A schedule of events giving details of times and places.

program book   A printed schedule of meeting events, location of function rooms, and other pertinent information which is usually the official program for the event.

program design   The structure of event program elements to achieve specific goals and objectives which includes the presentation method (format), topics, special events, free time, and breaks.

Program Evaluation and Review Techniques (PERT)   A graphic tool for providing organizational and personnel effectiveness using specific time segments as benchmarks.

program participant   See **participant.**

projection room   The area at the back or above an auditorium used for showing film and storing equipment.

projection screen   A front or rear surface on which images are displayed.

promotion   The publicizing of an event.

promotional fare   An airline fare offered below regular rates, usually with specific travel time limitations.

promoter   A person or organization whose role is to market an event by maximizing media coverage and income.

proof 1. A final copy for approval before printing; also known as **blueline.** 2. To correct before final printing. 3. A standard measure of alcoholic strength, e.g., 100 proof=50% alcohol content.

property A lodging establishment such as a hotel, motel, inn, resort, conference center, or event facility.

proposal A plan put forth for consideration or acceptance.

props Stage furniture, set dressing, and all articles used by actors or entertainers, or when used as room decorations known as decor.

proscenium An arch that separates the stage from the auditorium.

prospectus Site selection data and event specifications submitted to prospective facilities; also known as **exhibition prospectus.**

protection A reservation made on an alternate flight to ensure travel on a specific date.

protocol (prō-ta-KOL) Customs and regulations dealing with diplomatic formality, precedence, and etiquette.

provisional program See **preliminary program.**

provisional registration See **pending registration.**

PSA See **public service announcement.**

PTA See **prepaid ticket advice.**

public address system (PA) A system used to amplify sound into one or more rooms.

publications Printed items, such as books, magazines, newspapers, and conference documentation.

Publicity The activity of generating interest and attendance at an upcoming event by providing information with news value to the media to gain public attention or support; this process is controlled by the medium reporting the information, not the sponsor.

public relations 1. Presentation of an event via the media or other outlets, stressing the benefits and desirability of such an event. 2. A management function that evaluates public attitudes, identifies the policies and procedures of an individual or an organization with public interest, and plans and executes a program of action to earn public understanding and acceptance.

public service announcement (PSA) Free commercial space given by the media to non-profit organizations as available.

public show An exhibition open to the public usually requiring an entrance fee; see **consumer/trade show.**

public space Space in a facility that is available for public use.

purchase order See **payment order.**

push-pole tent A tent supported by a series of center, quarter, and side poles requiring guy ropes that must be secured to anchors or stakes in the ground.

pyro musical display A fireworks display staged to music.

pyrotechnician A person who is an expert in **pyrotechnics.**

pyrotechnics The art and science of designing, manufacturing, and displaying fireworks.

PZM See **boundary microphone** or **plate microphone.**

Q&A A question and answer period.

quad See **quadruple.**

quad box A set of four electrical outlets located in one box.

quadruple (quad) 1. A room with two or more beds for four persons. 2. A four-channel audio tape recording system.

quality control The discipline of maintaining quality.

quality management A business practice encompassing eight principles: leadership, policy and planning, information analysis, people, customer service, quality process, product and service, organizational performance.

quart A unit of measure equal to ¼ gallon, 32 ounces, or 4 cups.

quarter poles Tent poles positioned between the center and side poles, shorter than the center poles but taller than the side poles, which provide additional support, especially for tents 60' or wider.

quartz lamp A kind of high intensity projection light.

queen room A room with one queen-size bed suitable for one or two persons.

queen-size bed A large bed usually measuring 60" × 80" (150 cm × 200 cm).

quick-change booth An enclosed or draped area, close to the stage, for costume changes.

quorum (KWOR-um) A minimum number of members present to allow voting and official business to be conducted.

raw tape

rack rate A facility's standard, pre-established guest room rate.

radio See **walkie-talkie.**

radio microphone See **cordless/wireless microphone.**

rail A low drape divider between exhibit booths.

rain check The practice of setting another event date should the original be canceled.

rain date A contractual agreement which sets another event date if the original is cancelled due to poor weather.

rain insurance An insurance coverage which protects the financial interest of the sponsor or organizer in the event of a predetermined amount of rainfall.

R&B Rhythm and blues, a style of music.

rally A gathering to promote enthusiasm and excitement.

random access The ability to retrieve, in any sequence, visual and taped elements regardless of original placement order.

range rate The price of a **guest/sleeping room** based on a combination of minimum, middle, and maximum room rates. The number of rooms in each type varies.

rapporteur (**RAP-a-tour**) 1. A monitor who evaluates conference sessions. 2. A person appointed to record the proceedings of a session and to write a summary of the paper presented for a final summation session; also known as **reporter.**

rap sessions Informal sessions with no specific agenda.

raw footage The total collection of all film or videotape shot by a production crew from which the final product is generated.

raw tape A blank recording medium, ¼" to ½" in width, on reel, cartridge, or cassette, upon which material can be recorded.

RCMA See **Religious Conference Management Association.**

reader board See **function board.**

rear lit A technique for lighting a transparency from behind.

rear screen projection An image projected on the back surface of a screen which is placed between the viewer and the projector.

receding colors Colors on the right side of the color wheel such as blues and violets.

receiving line The dignitaries, host, sponsor, and guests of honor lined up to greet guests.

receiving line reception A stand-up social function with food and beverages.

reception A typically short social function with beverages, usually also with food displayed on tables for self-service or passed on trays.

reception desk/registration desk The area to which guests report upon arrival at an event or facility.

recession A withdrawing **procession.**

reel-to-reel See **tape recorder.**

refresh A general housekeeping activity of cleaning a room between sessions and after an event.

refreshment break The time between sessions when coffee and/or other refreshments are served; also known as **coffee break** or **break.**

refreshments Items of food and drink consumed between main meals and at **breaks** between meetings.

refund A reimbursement of money in the form of cash or credit voucher.

Religious Conference Management Association (RCMA)

refund policies A policy which determines the allowable reasons and timelines for the return of event fees in whole or part.

regional security officer (RSO) A consular official charged with the security of his/her country's nationals while they are traveling in his/her region; also known as **consular security manager.**

registrant A individual who has submitted a registration form and attends an event.

registrar An individual responsible for handling registrations.

registration 1. The process by which an individual indicates his intent to attend a conference or stay at a property. 2. The inclusion as a **participant** in an event; also a method of booking and payment.

registration card A signature form used by a facility when registering a guest.

registration card key A plastic card used in place of a room key; also see **computer card.**

registration fee The amount payable for attendance at a conference that may vary according to level of participation or type of membership.

registration kit A packet of event materials such as program book, tickets, maps, which may be given in advance or on-site at the event; also known as **registration packet.**

registration packet See **conference pack** or **registration kit.**

release forms 1. A form provided by management to permit removal of goods from exhibition. 2. A form signed by presenter allowing recording of presentation.

Religious Conference Management Association (RCMA) An organization providing information and resources to its members who are meeting planners for religious conventions, meetings, and assemblies and those who provide products and services for this industry.

religious meetings

religious meetings   Group gatherings which meet to discuss religious subjects.

remote control   Control of apparatus, such as audiovisual equipment, from a distance.

remote scanner   A scanning device placed at some distance from a laser to which laser light is fed by transmission fiber optics or a direct beam-shot, permitting more points of origin for laser effects without reusing additional lasers. Trade-offs are a loss of intensity and a flattening of the beam.

rendering   See **setup drawing.**

rental booth   A complete booth package offered to exhibitors on a rental basis.

rental charges   The cost of hiring a piece of equipment or an exhibit space which may or may not include ancillary services such as security, connections to water, electricity, gas.

rental specialist   A professional who specializes in providing equipment for events, including tables, chairs, tents, tableware, linen, stanchions, generators, and dance floors.

report   An informed, written record of a meeting.

reporter   See **rapporteur.**

representation   A statement made in the application for insurance that the prospective insured represents as being correct to the best of their knowledge.

reprise (re-PREEZ)   A repetition of the musical theme.

request for coverage   See **photo opportunity.**

request for proposal (RFP)   A request from the buyer of a service or a product to the potential supplier outlining all the requirements and necessary information for the supplier to prepare a bid; also known as **bid manual/specifications.**

reservation The process by which an individual or group secures space at a facility or books transportation.

reservation center The telephone reservation sales office.

reservation form See **hotel accommodation form.**

Resolution 1. The ability of a television system to distinguish and reproduce fine detail picked up by the camera. 2. A motion put forward for a joint decision.

résumé See **banquet event order** or **function sheet.**

retail event An event whose purpose is to introduce or sell merchandise to prospective customers.

retrace The return line from the end to the beginning of a graphic when a laser refreshes a drawing, visible if not *blanked*. Imagine that the laser is displaying a word; when the beam finishes the work, it jumps back to the beginning of the word to redraw it. This flyback, if not blanked, is seen as a **retrace** line.

return 1. A panel joined to backwall at right angles. 2. A reservation for a return journey.

reunions Events held for the purpose of bringing together groups for reminiscence who have past common interests and experiences. The most common of these are *school* and *military reunions* which bring together graduates of schools and military personnel who once served together; *family reunions* focus on bringing together family members living distances apart.

reverb See **effects device.**

reverse An effect produced by negative form of original type or art resulting in black or other color background with copy appearing in white or other color of paper on which it is printed.

RFP See **request for proposal.**

rider 1. A clause in an artist's contract stipulating special requirements for travel, dressing rooms, technical equipment; also known as **plus-plus**. 2. An insurance term for policy additions.

ridge The horizontal line or peak between the tops of the center poles in the roof of a tent.

rigger A skilled person used in handling assembly of heavy materials.

risers 1. Platforms of varying heights used together to create a performance stage. 2. Rows of steps used by entertainers during a performance. 3. Also known as **rostrum steps,** or **treads.**

risk An uncertainty arising from the possible occurrence of given events.

risk management The practice of analyzing all exposures to risk of loss by fortuitous or accidental means and taking steps to minimize those potential or real losses to levels acceptable to the organization.

roll-a-way A portable bed that can be provided for an extra person.

roll-in meal A light buffet meal served from a cart rolled directly into the room.

Roman candles A long paper tube packed with round stars and black powder; when lit the stars shoot out every four seconds to a height of about 75 feet.

room 1. A chamber used for lodging. 2. A place where an event is held.

rooming list A list of facility guests and room data supplied to facility prior to arrival.

room nights The number of rooms blocked or occupied multiplied by number of nights each room is reserved or occupied.

room rate The amount charged for the occupancy of a room.

room service A facility department which provides food and beverage service to guest rooms.

room setup The layout of tables, chairs, other furniture, and equipment for functions.

room, tax, and incidentals (RTI) The total hotel charge for accommodation, applicable taxes, and miscellaneous charges incurred by a guest.

rope lights A string of small, low-voltage lights inside a clear or colored transparent plastic tube run by a controller; also known as **tube lights**.

roping A plush-covered chain used to define traffic areas which can be attached to stanchions.

rostered times See **overtime**.

rostrum See **podium**.

rostrum steps See **risers**.

rough layout An artist's sketchy rendering of approximate placement of art and type or event room layout.

round A banquet table, usually 60" in diameter and available in 66" and 72" diameters.

round robin A contest or tournament in which each participant is matched with every other participant.

round slide tray See **carousel tray**.

roundtable A group of experts who meet on an equal basis to review and discuss specialized, professional matters, either in closed session or, more frequently, before an audience.

roving microphone/mike A small microphone, with or without wire, which can be moved easily through an audience for questions or comments.

RSO See **regional security officer**.

RTI See **room, tax, and incidentals**.

runner 1. A long, narrow carpet in a hallway, aisle, or on stage. 2. A piece of portable or constructed staging that extends a main stage to form a runway. 3. A main cord extending from a microphone to an amplifier. 4. An errand person available for assignment during an event or conference; also known as a **gofer**.

running order See **banquet event order**.

running schedule See **banquet event order**.

running sheet See **event order (EO)/running sheet/running order**.

run-of-the-house rate A rate for facility guest room block. Does not include suites; also known as **flat rate**.

run-through A complete rehearsal including all elements of the event or production, such as presentations, performances, music or entertainment, lighting, audio-visual, and technical aspects.

runway A platform that extends from the stage perpendicularly into the audience; also known as **catwalk**.

Russian service A style of banquet service where the waiter offers food from a silver platter to guests who help themselves.

S-Hook　See **sign hook**.

Saddle-stitch　A stapled or wired spine of a book or magazine.

SAG　See **Screen Actors Guild**.

sales manager　An individual who handles specific accounts and reports to the **director of sales**. See **director of sales**.

sales meeting　A meeting to introduce new products and their applications and to motivate sales staff.

sales promotions　A special event whose objective is to increase sales and customers.

salute　A fireworks shell filled with an aluminum mixture that produces a loud bang or noise.

satellite meeting　Meeting on a similar or a related subject taking place either concurrently or shortly before or after main event.

scanner or galvanometer (laser)　The mirror-bearing device used to guide a laser beam in programmable patterns. Each scanner includes a shaft that rotates within an electromagnetic field like a motor. Unlike a motor, however, the scanner shaft does not rotate a full 360 degrees but only slightly in one direction, or the other, that is, about 20 degrees plus, and 20 degrees minus, electric zero. The shaft of each scanner supports a mirror. The X mirror imparts horizontal positioning to the beam; the Y mirror imparts vertical positioning to the beam. The laser beam travels across both mirrors, allowing the beam to be aimed anywhere within an XY graphic field, thus, to draw pictures. The viewer sees imagery because the scanner repeats, or refreshes the drawing at least twenty times per second. Analogous to the frame rate of film or video, this rapid repetition creates the phenomenon of persistence.

scenario　A list showing all event details with their specific requirements: hour, date, and names of individuals involved and responsible per event; also known as **example** or **overview**.

school desks　Desks and chairs with attached writing surfaces; also known as **tablet chairs** or **writing chairs**.

schoolroom perpendicular setup

schoolroom perpendicular setup A configuration similar to a classroom with tables set perpendicular to the head table and chairs placed on both sides; also known as **union seating**.

schoolroom setup A configuration of tables lined in a row, one behind the other on each side of a center aisle with chairs facing the head table; also known as **classroom seating**.

scissor lift See **high jacker**.

SCMP See **Society of Corporate Meeting Planners**.

Sconce An ornamental wall bracket for candles or other lights.

scoop A **floodlight**.

scooter See **electric cart**.

score Sheet music provided to musicians showing all parts of the instruments or voices.

screen A front or rear projection surface. See **divider**.

Screen Actors Guild (SAG) The professional union representing actors and actresses.

screen/audience distance The distance between the projection screen and the front row of the audience.

screen/audience left and right Stage directions given from the audience perspective.

scrim 1. A translucent material used to diffuse or soften light. 2. Gauze-like theatrical curtains.

script A written text of program presentations.

scroll Copy or graphics which move slowly up the screen in video or film.

scroller/color changer A string of gels (up to 21) fitted in front of a lamp that can be programmed to be static in any color chosen or scrolled for an effect and operated from the **lighting desk**.

secateurs (Se-ca-TOURS) A cutter used by florists.

secretariat The clerical staff of an organization that sponsors an event.

secretary general The permanent head of a general organization that sponsors an event.

security A system developed and used to keep people and property safe, such as guards, closed circuit TV, etc.

security guard An armed, plain-clothed, or uniformed individual who is responsible for protecting an assigned area and may be hired from a privately operated company.

security service A service providing security protection, such as checking delegates credentials, searching hand luggage, protecting equipment, and patrolling congress and exhibition areas.

segue (SEG-way) A transition between two audio passages or video segments.

self-contained An entertainment act, group, or production that can supply its own sound, music, and lights.

self-contained exhibit An exhibit where crate is opened and becomes part of display.

seminar A lecture and dialogue allowing participants to share experiences in a particular field under the guidance of an expert discussion leader.

serpent In pyrotechnics, a short tube packed with a chemical mixture that propels the device with a strong jet flame in a zigzag or circular pattern.

serpentine A configuration of tables set in curving shapes, often S-shaped.

service charge A fee for the services of waiters/waitresses, housemen, technicians, and other food function personnel.

service contractor

service contractor   The **general contractor** for an exposition or convention.

service kit   A packet for exhibitors containing information and forms relating to the exhibition; also known as **exhibitor's kit** or **exhibitor manual**.

service level   1. The number of people one waiter is assigned to serve. 2. Type, coverage, and quality of services offered by a facility or contractor.

services and facilities   Items provided by or available from the event facility to enable the customer, delegate, or committee to get maximum benefits, such as the provision of secretarial services, cleaning, power, transportation, and catering.

session   A single uninterrupted segment of the conference program.

set   1. A performance area including props, equipment, and backdrops. 2. The length of time a band or orchestra plays between breaks. 3. To make preparations for a predetermined number of attendees. 4. To arrange type for printed materials.

set light   A light which illuminates background or **set** behind the performers.

set piece   In pyrotechnics, a wooden frame onto which a desired pattern or image is outlined with **lances**. A traditional Fourth of July set piece is the American flag. Sets can be very big and beautiful.

setup   1. The configuration of furniture within a function room. 2. Mixers, fruit, and glassware accompanying a liquor order.

setup drawing   A rendering that shows the installation procedure; also known as **rendering**.

setup personnel   Installers who construct exhibits, place furniture, and decorate the exhibition space.

setup time   The period of time necessary for the preparation of the event facility before the arrival of **participants**.

SGMP See **Society of Government Meeting Planners.**

shag A type of carpet.

shell In pyrotechnics, a paper container filled with stars or other fireworks ingredients, such as comets, hummingbirds, lances, serpents, or whistles, designed to form a pattern or effect when displayed; they are either round or cylindrical, depending on whether the manufacturer is Asian or Italian.

shell folder A brochure with preprinted illustrations to which varying text can be added.

shell scheme A European **booth/stand** system which usually includes a raised floor, back and side walls, and **fascia.**

sherbet glasses A short glass serving dish with foot and stem used for serving ices and desserts.

shoehorn A term meaning overcrowding of a hotel; also known as **gridlock.**

S-hook See **sign hook.**

shot A one-ounce measurement of liquor.

shotgun microphone See **hyper-cardioid microphone.**

shoulder The intermediate time in the tourism industry between **peak** and **low seasons.**

show card A material used for making signs.

show manager A person responsible for all aspects of an exhibition or trade show; also known as **exhibition manager.**

show office The management office at an exhibition.

show photographer The official photographer for an event appointed by manager.

show plate A decorative plate preset at each banquet guest place and removed at start of service; also known as an **underliner.**

show producer A company or individual who initiates and plans an event and responsible for renting a site and soliciting participants.

show tape See **production tape.**

shutter In laser technology, an attachment that blocks the laser beam, usually from exiting the projector.

shuttle service Transport facilities for participants, usually by coach or van.

side chair An armless chair.

side fills Speakers located stage right and stage left used to project amplified sound to the full stage area.

side poles The support poles placed around the perimeter of a tent; also known as **pin poles.**

side rail A low divider wall in exhibit area.

side stitch binding A binding process by which folded sections of a book or magazine are placed on top of one another and stitched together from top to bottom.

side walls Detachable canvas or plastic walls used to create the sides of a tent.

sight acts Performers who must be watched to be appreciated, such as mimes, jugglers, dancers, and acrobats; also known as **incidental entertainment,** and **variety artists.**

sight line See **line of sight.**

sightseeing tour An excursion to points of interest often by bus or van.

signage All informational and directional signs required for an event.

signaling system A system of communication between the speaker and the projectionist or the chairman and the speaker.

signal-to-noise ratio The ratio of the video or audio signal to the noise interference accompanying that signal.

signatory See **authorized signature.**

sign cloth A lightweight material, as opposed to canvas, used for banners, signs, and streamers.

sign holder A stand for displaying signs.

sign hook A piece of S-shaped metal for hanging signs; also known as **S-hook.**

significant other A person who serves an important personal role in another's life; often used to denote the companion of an invited guest at an event when the companion is not a spouse.

signs Informational displays used at events; see **banner.**

sign service A service which provides **signs** for exhibitors.

sign standard A frame on a stand.

silverprint See **blueline.**

simultaneous interpretation The process of orally translating one language into another or signing for the deaf while a person is speaking; also known as **consecutive interpretation.**

single In entertainment, one musician or performer.

single bed A bed measuring 38" × 75" (95 cm × 188 cm); also known as **twin bed.**

single room A guest room occupied by one person.

single-source sound A sound produced by placing a large cluster of speakers at a single location; usually high to medium in volume level and best used for performances requiring an audio focal point; also known as **point source.**

SITE See **Society of Incentive Travel Executives.**

site An area, property, or specific facility to be used for an event.

site inspection A personal, careful investigation of a property, facility, or area, prior to the event.

skewing A zig-zag pattern on a TV screen due to improper head alignment.

skid A low, small platform used for storing and transporting merchandise; also known as **pallet.**

skip A departing guest who fails to pay for accommodations.

skirting A decorative covering around tables or risers.

sky cap An airport porter who handles baggage.

slide A photographic transparency mounted on a small plastic frame or film arranged for projection; also known as **two-by-two.**

slide animation A technique that creates the illusion of movement of an image when a series of slides are projected in rapid sequence.

slider A telescopic pipe enabling one section to slide inside another and used with draping to allow various widths and lengths.

SMERF A "catch all" category of meeting market segments including social, military, educational, religious, and fraternal groups.

smoke generation The creation of fog using chemicals and heat. A *dry-ice machine* is a 30 to 55 gallon drum containing a heating element and an exhaust fan. When dry ice (frozen carbon dioxide) is submerged in hot water, the machine produces a fog that is forced out of the machine by a fan and directed through a 4" diameter vent hose. Dry ice fog is low-lying, producing a fog close to the ground. **Burn units** use a non-carbon liquid chemical and are about the size of a bread box. The liquid is heated in the unit and the resulting fog is expelled under pressure toward the desired area. Older **burn units** use petroleum-based fluids which produce a noxious odor and slippery residue; **burn units** are the most practical way to create fog or smoke in mid-air; the fog is often referred to as Rosco fog, named after Rosco Laboratories, the major supplier of the chemical fluid used.

SMPTE timecode A numeric code developed and approved by the Society of Motion Picture and Television Engineers (SMPTE) to identify individual frames in film and video.

snifter A large, short-stemmed goblet used for **cordials,** cognac, and brandy.

social dinner A non-working evening function at which a meal is served.

social events A lifecycle celebration such as **weddings, bar/bas mitzvahs, anniversaries, birthdays,** etc.

society music Dance or period music of the 1930s, 1940s, and 1950s.

Society of Corporate Meeting Planners (SCMP) An organization providing information and resources to its members who coordinate corporate meetings and those who provide services and products for this industry.

Society of Government Meeting Planners (SGMP) An organization providing information and resources to its members who coordinate events for government agencies and those who provide services and products for this industry.

Society of Incentive Travel Executives (SITE) An organization providing information and resources to its members who coordinate corporate incentive programs and products for this industry.

soft opening A period of time when a new facility is open for business prior to the grand opening.

software Computer programs that cause equipment to "think" in a particular format.

sound board A **console** with separate channels to control volume and sound quality produced by each **microphone;** also known as **mixing board,** and **console.**

sound effects Recorded or live sounds used for special theatrical audio effects.

soundproof wall A barrier, usually permanent, that prevents sound from carrying to and from adjacent rooms.

soundscaping A composition of recorded audio that creates a particular mood.

sound slidetray See **carousel tray.**

sound system An electric audio speaker system used to amplify sound.

sound/video bite A short sound or visual message which summarizes the major point of a story.

sound wings Risers on stage right and stage left for stacked sound equipment that allow storage space hidden from the audience's view; also known as **speaker platforms.**

space assignment Booth space assigned to exhibiting companies.

space rate The cost per square foot for space rental.

space reservation form A form to officially request to utilize a particular space.

spark pot A pyrotechnic device that emits a burst of sparks, usually silver, when ignited.

speaker 1. A person who presents an address on a specific topic or topics, including keynote; general session and seminar leader who are topic specialists; a trainer and workshop leader who allows for group participation and interaction; and "change of pace" speaker such as humorists and entertainers. 2. A mechanical transducer that converts electrical impulses back into sound waves; the output source of all sound systems. 3. A device for talent to hear music on stage.

speaker platforms Risers on the right and left of stage used to elevate sound equipment; see **sound wings.**

speaker's guidelines Instructions regarding the required format to be used for the written preparation of a speech.

speakers' room/lounge An area with audiovisual equipment for speakers to prepare prior to or between speeches.

spec book Written specifications, requirements, and instructions for all functions, room setups, services, and purveyors which includes names of key personnel, their areas of responsibility, special events, and any other related information; also see **staging guide.**

special A light focused on a particular area of a room or stage.

special-effects editing The electronic assembly of film or videotape using **dissolves, fades, wipes,** or other unusual visual manipulation of an image. It can be used to create or sustain a mood or to join segments of a presentation that would not ordinarily match, and can only be accomplished in an **on-line edit** suite.

special lighting In film and video production, lighting equipment that exceeds what a typical two-person video crew would carry and is used to create special effects, moods, or alter existing lighting; examples include spotlights and strobes.

special rate An amount charged for the occupancy of a room, usually at a reduced rate and negotiated as a **group rate** by the conference organizers.

special-rate package A lowered, all-inclusive rate, frequently including one or more meals for two or three nights, that is offered to the general public; often used to generate off-season or weekend business.

specifications A complete written description of event requirements; also see **request for proposal.**

spike marks Tape or chalk marks on studio or stage floors designating exact placement of props and actors; also known as **marks.**

split charter Two or more groups sharing the same flight.

splits A small bottle containing about half the usual quantity of liquor.

split screen A horizontal or vertical separation of video images shown simultaneously.

splitter In laser technology, an attachment that divides the beam into two parts according to power, not color.

spokesperson A designated representative who has the authority, knowledge, and credibility to speak to and be interviewed by the media.

sponsor 1. One who assumes all or part of the financial responsibility for an event. 2. A commercial sponsor that provides financial backing for an aspect(s) of an event and who in return receives visibility, advertising, or other renumeration in lieu of cash.

sponsored bar See **open bar.**

sponsoring bodies An organization or institution which endorses an event often by financially underwriting all or a portion of an event.

sport event An event where athletes compete and spectators view the athletic activities and ceremonies.

spotlight A movable light focusing upon a particular person or object.

spot rehearsal A practiced run-through of any segment of a production.

spouse A husband or wife of an event attendee; also known as **accompanying person.**

spouse programs Educational and/or social events planned for **spouses** and guests of event **participants.**

sprinkler One overhead water outlet which is an element in a fire extinguishing system.

sprinkler system A fire protection system consisting of multiple overhead water outlets set to respond automatically in the case of fire.

Sprintmail An e-mail system provided by Sprintnet; also see **Telemail.**

squib or fuse head An electrical igniter used to initiate a pyrotechnic effect.

squirrel cage/barrel Spinning drum used for selecting winning raffle tickets for a drawing.

stacking chairs Chairs that save space by stacking on top of each other.

stage call 1. A notice to performers to gather at a certain time and place for a review of responsibilities. 2. To ask a celebrity or speaker to return to the stage after completing a presentation.

stage left, stage right A description of directions from the perspective of one who faces the audience from the stage.

stage lighting Lighting designated for the stage area only.

stage manager A person responsible for supervising the stage area including speakers, entertainers, technicians, and others.

stage maroon A pyrotechnical device that produces a very loud "bang" when ignited.

stage master See **stage manager.**

stage plot A diagram, drawn to scale, indicating placement on stage of artists' equipment, props, and microphones.

staging 1. The design and placement of elements for an event. 2. The implementation of an event.

staging area An area adjacent to main event area for setup, dismantling, and temporary storage.

staging guide A compilation of function sheets, scripts, instructions, room setup diagrams, directory of key personnel, forms, and other material relating to the event; also see **spec book.**

stakes Pointed pegs used to secure the guy ropes of a tent in the ground. Wooden stakes are used for grass-covered earth steel stakes are required when the ground is extremely hard, rocky, or paved; also known as **anchors.**

stanchions Decorative upright bars, or posts, which hold markers, flags, or ropes to define traffic areas at gatherings.

stand   A European term for **booth;** see **booth.**

standby   An attempt to travel on a flight without a confirmed reservation.

stand-in   A person substituting for a performer, speaker, or VIP.

standing committee   A permanent committee, defined by organizational bylaws, which meets to conduct its specific responsibilities.

standing microphone   A microphone attached to an adjustable vertical floor stand.

stars   In pyrotechnics, the colored fire produced by a mixture of fine-grade chemicals that appears when a fireworks shell displays in the night sky; may be round (the size of a dime) or square (the size of a sugar cube) depending on the manufacturer—Asian or Italian.

statement of account   A financial report of income and expenses.

stats   The photographic material used in preparing camera-ready art; also known as **photo stats,** or **velox.**

stay-over   A guest who stays at facility beyond stated departure date.

steering committee   A group of individuals created by an organization who set policies and make basic decisions relative to a group or an event.

stet   A proofreading term noted when copy marked for deletion is to be put back in its original form.

stop motion   See **freeze frame.**

storyboard   A series of rough sketches that depict the scene and action in a planned film or program; see **field production.**

straight time   Labor performed and paid at standard rate for work during normal business hours as established by unions.

street beat   A drum beat accompanying a band that is marching but not playing.

strike 1. A collective refusal to work by union workers, also known as a **walkout.** 2. To remove all scenery and props from stage. 3. To dismantle and remove an exhibit.

strip To put a negative into place as part of a larger or composite negative in preparing to make an offset printing plate.

striplight A long, narrow fixture with a row of lamps, often with reflectors and color gels, used in color lighting.

strobe lights An electronic lighting instrument that emits extremely rapid but brief flashes of brilliant light; with better models, the range and intensity of these flashes can be adjusted. When the flash rate is properly adjusted, it is possible to create the illusion of slow motion. Requires posting of caution signs to alert event participants of usage.

stub space See **feeder space.**

studio A guest room with couches that convert to beds.

study mission See **educational visit.**

stuffing The repetitive act of placing assembled written materials in an envelope, folder, or other presentation packet.

subcommittee A group of people, frequently including one or more members of the main committee, meeting outside of the main committee, with responsibilities for specific items.

subcontractor A company retained by **general contractor** or **event manager** to provide services or products.

suite A **parlor** with one or more guest rooms.

summary/brief A written short version of speech or paper; also known as an **abstract.**

summary of discussions A short report of discussions that have taken place in the event hall.

summary record/report A short account of a speech, debate, or discussion.

super-APEX fare An airline **APEX fare** at a lower rate but with more restrictions.

superimposition The projection of two images on a screen at the same time.

supervisor See **banquet captain, maitre d'**.

supper The evening meal; also known as **dinner**.

supplemental airline A non-scheduled airline.

supplier A facility, company, agency, or person offering space, goods, or services.

surcharge A charge over and above established rates.

survey An evaluation tool used to collect exhibitors' opinions regarding services or attendees' reactions to an event.

switcher 1. The engineer, or technical director, who changes from video camera to video camera. 2. A panel with rows of buttons and levers that allows shifting from one camera or sound source to another.

SWOT analysis An analytical tool used to forecast the potential benefits and deficits of a future event based on the strengths, weaknesses, opportunities, and threats of past or comparable events.

symposium 1. A meeting or conference at which experts discuss a particular subject and express opinions. 2. A meeting of a number of experts in a particular field, at which papers are presented and discussed by specialists with a view to making recommendations.

synchronization The recording of sound and image at the same time.

table d'hôte (TA-bl'-DOT) A meal served at a fixed price which in some areas may be served by a waiter.

table microphone A microphone on a short stand placed on a table for seated speakers.

table service A style of banquet service at which guests are served, at each course, a full plate with every item already on it.

tablet chairs See **school desks.**

tabletent A small sign used to identify the speaker or speakers.

table top display A portable display that can be set up on top of a table.

table top presentation A small exhibit on tables often used in combination with posters.

table wine A class of wines fermented to about 12 to 14 percent alcohol.

T & T An abbreviation used to signal tax and tip.

taffeta A stiff, lustrous fabric used for skirting or special draping.

talent Entertainers or performers used in an event.

talent/booking agent A representative for talent who locates and contracts for bookings for events.

talk An electronic service that allows two users logged onto the **Internet** to communicate with each other in real time.

talkback A speaker system that connects the director's control room with the studio.

tally light A small red light on a television camera that notifies the talent when the camera is on.

tally sheet A form used to keep track of the number of rooms sold and/those still available; also used to account for event attendees, equipment, etc.

tap A device used for starting or stopping the flow of beverage from a container.

tape deck   See **tape recorder**.

tape recorder   A device for recording and playing back audio signals from a tape medium; the most cost-effective means of providing prerecorded material for events; also known as a **tape deck.** Audio tapes can be of three types. A *cartridge* is a ¼" closed-loop tape with one or two tracks, which automatically recycles and is of broadcast standard. It is used for special effects such as prerecorded announcements and is semi-automated. A *cassette* is a ¼" tape in a closed case with one to four tracks, which can be a continuous loop, auto repeating, and automated. It is the standard product for broadcast music and prerecorded shows. A *reel-to-reel* tape is an open-reel tape of one-quarter to two inches in width, with one to thirty-two tracks for recording.

tare weight   The weight of a container and/or packing materials deducted from the total weight to determine the weight of the contents or load.

TCP/IP   See **Transmission Control Protocol/Internet Protocol.**

teach-in   A session specially held for the application of modifications and additions necessary to keep a particular subject up-to-date.

teardown   The dismantling of equipment at the conclusion of an event.

teasers   1. Vertical side curtains that, when combined with a horizontal **tormentor** curtain, frame a stage. 2. A promotional piece designed to build interest in an event.

tech check   A confirmation that all the technical aspects of a production or event are in working condition.

technical director   A trained individual who calls for cues for a performance.

technical meeting   Groups whose members and suppliers work in scientific, research, or applied sciences; United States/Canada: non-medical meetings of professional organizations.

theater setup

technical rehearsal A run-through of the technical aspects of a show, including lighting, sound, and special effects.

technical visit A tour by conference participants to a work place related to their particular interests.

teleconference A type of event that brings together three or more people in two or more locations through telecommunications; *audioconference* refers to audio only, such as a telephone; *videoconferencing* refers to a combined audio and visual link through satellite or other type of network.

Telemail Sprintmail used to be called Telemail because Sprintnet used to be called Telenet. See **Sprintmail.**

Telnet A program on the **Internet** that provides support for a variety of terminals to allow for logging into a network from a remote location.

teleprompter An electronic device that allows a display of script to aid a speaker or performer.

telescopic pipe A drape support where one section slides inside another for use at various lengths. See **sliders.**

tension structure A tent designed to have all perimeter loading equally distributed over a series of **catenary arches,** which provides greater stability.

tent A portable canvas or vinyl shelter for an outside function.

tentative hold A space temporarily held by a facility pending a definite booking; also known as **option.**

tent specialist Rental specialist who rents and installs tents for events.

terminal A freight handling at dock area or at an airport.

theater setup A configuration of chairs, set up in rows facing the head table, stage, or speaker; variations are semicircular and V-shaped; also known as **auditorium setup.**

theme break A break during formal program sessions with special food and beverages pertaining to a theme and often including decorations, costumes, and entertainment.

theme party The invitation, food, decorations, entertainment, and other elements all relate to a central concept.

third party policy See **automobile liability insurance.**

throw A projection distance for lighting or audiovisual.

TIAA See **Travel Industry Association of America.**

ticket revalidation A technique of amending an airline ticket to reflect new flights booked.

tiered The arrangement of rows of chairs, one above the other.

timber-battens See **batten (bats).**

time and materials A method of charging for services and materials used on a cost-plus basis.

timecode The sequential numbers assigned to each frame of video or film representing the passage of time in hours, minutes, seconds, and even tenths of seconds—for example, 01:20:35:10, which indicates that this frame can be found in the first hour, twentieth minute, thirty-fifth second, and first tenth of a second of the videotape or film. Time codes are used for catalog purposes when identifying scenes and are most important during editing, saving valuable time in locating scenes needed for a particular edit.

time delay The length of time between the production of live sound and when it is actually heard.

time draft A draft which matures a specified number of days after acceptance or after the date of the draft.

timeline See **production schedule.**

tip An amount of money given to service workers to show appreciation; also known as **gratuity.**

transfer

titles Written or graphic materials shown on camera, such as credits.

toastmaster See **MC**

tormentor The horizontal curtain that runs from stage right to left connecting the vertical curtains called **teasers.**

tour See **excursion.**

tour-based fares A reduced rate excursion fare available to those who buy prepaid tours or packages.

tower A vertical, metal structure used to hold lighting equipment above a performance area.

tow motor See **forklift.**

track lighting Lighting attached to a rodlike metal track mounted on a ceiling or wall which allows for flexible spotlighting and other lighting effects.

trade A line of work or occupation pursued as a business such as **event management.**

trade show An exhibition of products and services sometimes open to the public but often only open to registered attendees; also known as **industrial show, exhibition, exposition.**

trade show organizer Individual who plans a trade show, reserves the space, markets to exhibitors, and promotes attendance by buyers.

traffic flow 1. The movement of people through an area. 2. Movement of vehicles around a venue.

trainer An instructor of techniques and skills on a specific subject.

training meeting A structured learning session in which a teacher presents specific information and techniques.

transcription A written copy of spoken material.

transfer The process of moving equipment and/or people from one point to another.

transient space A short-term rental space.

transit A passenger changing planes without going through security or customs.

transit visa A government-issued permit allowing its holder to stop over in a country to make a travel connection or for a brief visit.

translation A conversion of one language to another, orally or in writing.

translation service Translating written material or conversation from one language to another.

Transmission Control Protocol/Internet Protocol (TCP/IP) The system that networks use to communicate with each other. Software packages for hooking up the **Internet** are based on TCP/IP.

transmission fibers/fibres Fiber optics used for light or information transmission; also known as **fiber optics**.

transparencies An image on a plastic sheet or roll, clear or colored, viewed by projecting from an overhead projector to a screen.

transport See **cartage**.

transport coordinator/officer A person in charge of planning and managing transportation arrangements for participants.

travel agent (agency) A person or firm qualified to arrange for hotel rooms, meals, transportation, cruises, tours, and other travel requirements.

traveler A large curtain that opens horizontally from the middle or from one side of the stage.

Travel Industry Association of America (TIAA) An organization comprised of individuals and organizations in the United States travel industry whose purpose is to conduct research and promote travel products and services.

tray service See **butler service (American)**.

twin room

treads See **risers**.

trestle table A rectangular table ranging from 4' to 12' in length and 2½' in width.

triple sheet A bed made with a third sheet on top of the blanket.

trip tray A box rigged to empty its contents, such as snow or confetti, onto a stage.

troubleshoot The activity of identifying potential or existing problems and repairing malfunctions.

truck loaders Union labor specifically responsible for unloading equipment.

truss A structure of steel bars used to suspend lighting or other technical equipment over a stage.

T-shape setup A configuration of tables arranged in the shape of a block T with chairs set around all but the head table.

tube lights A string of small, low-voltage lights contained in a clear or transparent colored plastic tube, generally wired to be run by a three- or four-circuit sequencer (controller); used as a highlighter around signs, stages, or entrances. They can be bent and mounted on peg-board or other surfaces to form lighted words; also known as **rope lights**.

tunnel A horizontal cone of light produced by lasers and fog.

turn-down service A service in which beds are prepared for sleeping and usually includes replacement of bathroom linens.

turnover The time required to break down and reset an event.

turntable A motorized rotating platform.

twin bed A bed measuring 38" × 75" (95 cm x 88 cm). Also known as **single bed**.

twin double room A room occupied by two people.

twin room A room with two twin beds suitable for two persons.

two-by-two

two-by-two A piece of 35 mm photographic film usually in a 2" × 2" cardboard, glass, or plastic mount; also known as **slide.**

type face The name of a type design, e.g., Helvetica, Schoolbook, Times Roman, etc.

utility box

UCT   See **Universal Coordinated Time.**

underliner   See **show plate.**

underscore   To play music during a video or film scene.

unexpected departure   A guest who leaves facility before the stated departure date.

unidirectional microphone   A microphone that is sensitive to sound coming from the direction in which it is pointed.

union call   The number of union members hired to work an event.

union seating   See **schoolroom perpendicular setup.**

union steward   An on-site union official.

Universal Coordinated Time (UCT)   A standard for time whose master clock is maintained by the United States National Observatory in Bethesda, Maryland; see **Greenwich Mean Time** or **Zulu Time.**

up-linking   The sending of video signals via microwave to an existing satellite for transmission to selected sites or anyone capable of satellite reception for that signal; used for teleconferencing or broad distribution of a message on a national or international basis.

upper case   Capital letters.

upstage   The part of the stage farthest from the audience or camera.

Usenet   A very large electronic **bulletin board system** of thousands of discussion groups and forums about a broad range of topics.

U-shaped setup   A configuration of chairs arranged in a U shape that faces the head table or speaker; also known as **horseshoe setup** or **open-U setup.**

utility box   An area in a floor, wall, or column which houses electric outlets and other utility sources.

very important person (VIP)

valance   1. A trim or finish curtain, usually 12" deep with a scalloped edge, used to give a tent a finished appearance. 2. Overhead border used as a light **baffle**. 3. A trim used to dress the top of a projection screen.

value-added tax (VAT)   A tax which is levied at each stage of the production or distribution of a product and becomes a sales tax to the consumer.

van shipment   A shipment within a moving van of large pieces of furniture or display material which may be crated or uncrated.

vapor lights   Special effects lighting of high intensity.

variety artists   See **sight acts**.

variety entertainment   Singers, dancers, comics, or other performers with unique skills such as jugglers, magicians, clowns, or acrobats.

VAT   See **value-added tax**.

VCR   See **video cassette recorder**.

vega   See **cordless/wireless microphone**.

Velcro   A multi-purpose hook and loop material used for fastening.

velour   A velvety fabric with a nap.

velox   See **stats**.

vendor   A person who sells and provides services or products.

venue   Events physical site.

Veronica   A service on the **Internet** that helps make **Gopher** information searches easier and more manageable.

very important person (VIP)   An organization's officers, celebrity speakers, panel moderators, industry experts, or others who are distinguished from the majority in attendance.

VHS A videotape recorder and player utilizing the ½" VHS format; not compatible with **Beta** format.

video cassette recorder (VCR) A device used for audio and video recording; also see **video tape recorder.**

video character generator A computer-assisted device used to generate and create letters, numbers, and symbols electronically. In simple terms, it is a video typewriter used to create captions or text that is superimposed over a video image; it can also be used to recap key points made by a speaker or supply basic information, such as final credits.

video conferencing See **teleconference.**

video enhancement, or video magnification The enlargement of a video image from the size of a typical consumer television screen to dimensions for large projection screens used when attempting to present a larger-than-life image to an audience so that everyone can see close-up expressions and action.

video projection Projection of video productions by monitors or on large screen.

video tape recorder (VTR) An electronic device used for audio and video recording; also see **video cassette recorder (VCR).**

vinyl A plastic material used for drapes, skirting, banners, paneling, flooring, or covering table tops.

VIP See **very important person.**

VIP identification A means for identifying the very important people at an event using badges, flowers, or special seating.

visa A government endorsement stamped inside a passport by an official of the country the traveler wishes to visit allowing entrance for a specified period of time.

voluntary upgrade 1. The act in which a passenger moves to higher priced class for additional fare vouchers. 2. Tickets which travelers exchange for prepaid services such as accommodations, meals, and tours.

V-shaped setup A configuration of chairs arranged in rows, separated by a center aisle, slanted in a V shape facing the head table or speaker. Also known as a **chevron** or **herringbone setup.**

VTR See **video tape recorder.**

water cooling

Wais A service on the **Internet** that can be used to gather information about a topic from various locations and provide easier access to the information.

waiver of indemnity The intentional or voluntary relinquishment of responsibility for payment for damage, loss, or expense incurred by another party.

walk A term indicating a guest holding a confirmed reservation but sent to another facility because of **overbooking.**

walkie-talkie A mobile, wireless radio that transmits and receives oral communications; also known as **radio.**

walk-in A term indicating a guest requesting accommodations without a reservation.

walk-in/out music 1. Music accompanying arriving and exiting guests at an event; also known as **cocktail music.** 2. Music accompanying guests receiving awards; also known as **chaser music.**

walk out See **strike.**

walk-through Physical venue inspection.

warm-up An activity used to liven up the audience prior to show time.

wash light Broad, even light that softly illuminates all or part of a room or stage created by a group of floodlights (usually **PARs** or **fresnels**), used to provide general illumination of one or several colors. More than one wash can be set up to cover an area, allowing not only for a choice of colors by changing washes, but also for the creation of a wide range of colors by blending the washes.

waste removal The disposal of trash often accomplished by a contracted environmental specialist.

water closet (W.C.) A bathroom with toilets.

water cooling The method used to cool high-power lasers which requires a standard water supply (such as a janitor's sink drain).

In some circumstances the water is maintained in a closed system and the heat is extracted by a heat exchanger.

water stations Tables with pitchers of water and glasses for self service.

W.C. See **water closet.**

wedding A religious or legal ceremony of marriage often accompanied by social celebrations.

welcome cocktail A drink served as an introductory gesture of welcome which refers to a single drink or a reception where such drinks are served.

welcome reception An opening event at which drinks and food are served.

wet lease The rental of a plane with crew, supplies, fuel, and maintenance service.

whispered interpretation An interpretation in a low voice to participants, usually sitting next to the interpreter.

whistles In pyrotechnics, **serpents** with loud, multi-tone whistles.

white page directory A resource providing electronic address listings for users on the **Internet.**

white tie **Formal dress** requiring white tie and tails for men and formal evening dress for women.

wholesaler, tour A company which packages various components of tours and travel programs for sale through travel agencies.

windscreen A porous foam cover for microphones to block unwanted sound.

wings The off-stage area out of audience sight lines.

wipe A scene in a motion picture that appears to be pushed off screen by a new scene.

wired system interpretation A system to communicate interpretation by electric cables or wires.

wireless microphone See **cordless microphone.**

wishbone leg Fold-up leg on a display table.

work lights Lighting used for rehearsal or technical work on stage.

working drawing A detail drawing.

workshop 1. A training session in which participants develop skills and knowledge in a given field. 2. An event designed to stimulate intensive discussion and compensate for diverging views in a particular discipline or subject. 3. An informal public session of free discussion organized to take place between formal plenary sessions on a subject chosen by the participants or on a special problem suggested by the organizers.

world's fair An infrequently occurring celebrated that typically showcases the latest or future advances in the arts, culture, and technology.

World Wide Web (WWW) A compendium of information sources and libraries available through the **Internet;** a tool for providing access to **hypertext**-based information.

wrap-up 1. To conclude an event. 2. To prepare the final report on an event.

writing chair A chair with an attached writing surface; also known as **school desks,** or **tablet chairs.**

WWW See **World Wide Web.**

Xenon Lamp An extremely high-intensity light source for projection.

yield 1. Number of pieces kept from any given unit. 2. Number of usable servings per raw unit.

zones The rightmost part of an **Internet** address is called its zone. *Name zones* are divided into two categories: the three-letter kind and the two-letter kind. Three-letter zones are set up by type of organization. Example: *com* represents commercial organizations; *edu* stands for educational institutions; *gov* represents government bodies and departments. Within the United States, most **Internet** sites have names in one of the three-letter zones; elsewhere, it is more common to use geographic names, by country or other recognized political entity.

zoom lens Projection or camera lens of variable magnification that permits a smooth change of subject coverage between distance and close-up without changing the projection or the camera position.

Zulu Time **Greenwich Mean Time,** the world time standard; see **universal coordinated time (UCT).**

VAN NOSTRAND REINHOLD VNR

Your Name _____ Address _____
Title _____ City/State/Zip _____
Function _____ Phone _____
Company _____ Fax _____
Date of book purchase _____ E-Mail _____

Thank you for your interest in Van Nostrand Reinhold publications. To enable us to keep you abreast of the latest developments in your field, please complete the following information.

1. With respect to the topic of this book, are you a:
   a. student in this field
      name of your institution: _____
   b. working professional in this field
   c. hobbyist in this field

2. For how many years have you worked/studied in this field?
   _____

3. Of which professional associations are you a member?
   _____
   _____
   _____

4. To which industry or general food-related publications/resources do you subscribe for important information?
   _____
   _____
   _____

5. Describe your professional title:
   a. chef   h. sommelier
   b. caterer   i. consulting services
   c. restaurant owner/manager   j. government
   d. food and beverages manager   k. librarian
   e. student   l. education/research
   f. professor/teacher   m. other (please specify)
   g. pastry chef   _____

6. How/where was this book purchased? (circle one)
   a. bookstore
   b. publisher's outlet
   c. through offer in mail
   d. through book club
   e. other _____

7. How/where do you usually purchase professional books?
   (please circle all that apply)
   a. bookstore
   b. publisher's outlet
   c. through offer in mail
   d. through book club
   e. other _____

8. Do you own or have access to a computer with a modem?
   a. yes   b. no

9. To which electronic on-line services do you have access?
   (please circle all that apply)
   a. America On-Line   e. World Wide Web
   b. Prodigy   f. other (please specify)
   c. Compuserve   _____
   d. Internet   g. none

10. Do you own or have access to a computer with a CD-ROM reader?
    a. yes   b. no

11. Would you purchase updates, supplements and/or additional chapters to this book in an electronic format?
    a. yes   b. no

12. Which format would you prefer?
    a. disk (circle one)   Mac   Dos   Windows
    b. CD-ROM
    c. online
    d. other _____

13. What was the primary reason for purchasing this book?
    a. professional enrichment
    b. academic coursework
    c. personal interest/hobby
    d. other _____

14. Would you be interested in or subscribe to a Professional Chef's Newsletter?
    a. yes   b. no
    If yes, which do you prefer?
    a. online   b. print

15. In which of the following areas would you be interested in new books?
    a. International cuisine   e. buffets
    b. catering   f. wines
    c. baking and pastry   g. other (please specify)
    d. beverage management   _____

16. Please indicate author/title and ISBN# of book purchased:
    _____
    _____

VNR is constantly evaluating its services to better meet your needs. If you need further information please contact us by fax at **212-475-2548**.
BE SURE TO VISIT US AT OUR WEB SITE
http://www.vnr.com/vnr.html

ITP

BUSINESS REPLY MAIL
FIRST CLASS MAIL   PERMIT NO. 704   NEW YORK NY

POSTAGE WILL BE PAID BY ADDRESSEE

VAN NOSTRAND REINHOLD
Culinary and Hospitality
115 FIFTH AVENUE
4th Floor
NEW YORK, NY 10211-0025

NO POSTAGE
NECESSARY
IF MAILED
IN THE
UNITED STATES